In a culture drunk on dopamine hits, addicted to the adrenaline of achievement, and chasing the next shiny algorithm of happiness, Chris Maxwell offers us something revolutionary: the courage to stop. This isn't another book about getting more out of life—it's about discovering that life has already given us more than we know.

Maxwell writes like a poet who has walked through fire and emerged not bitter, but better. His words don't just teach; they heal. Contentment is both ancient wisdom and urgent medicine for our restless age. This book is a psalm for the overwhelmed, a prayer for the perpetually busy, and a love letter to anyone who has ever wondered if they're enough.

Discover what Maxwell already knows: the treasure you've been seeking has been buried in your own backyard all along. Bravo, Chris: you've gifted us a compass for the contented life.

—Leonard Sweet
author, professor, preacher, publisher,
proprietor of sanctuaryseaside.com

We're bombarded by promises that if we just achieve more things or acquire more stuff, we'll finally be happy. But at the heart of Chris Maxwell's new book is a radical notion—that contentment is received, not achieved. That it's something available in the present, as he writes, "in the sacred soil of our real lives." Chris leads the "quiet rebellion" by mining biblical wisdom to explain how to open your life to contentment, even amid trials and disappointments. You couldn't ask for a better guide. The topic is not merely theoretical for Chris. He's experienced more than his share of challenges, and he describes the journey to contentment in ways that are both honest and inspiring. I hope many join him on the voyage and discover the contentment God has been offering all along.

—Drew Dyck
Publishing professional
author, *Just Show Up*,
Your Future Self Will Thank You

In a world where comparison exhausts us and striving never seems to satisfy, Chris Maxwell offers us a different way. With honesty born out of his own suffering and wisdom drawn from decades of ministry, he reminds us that contentment is not a prize to win but a presence to receive. It is an invitation to let go of grasping and to receive all that we need from the One who is holding it all together. This is not theory—it is testimony. It is a map for weary pilgrims who long to discover that in Christ, enough has already been given. Chris has written a book that is as timely as it is timeless, and one that I believe will shepherd many hearts toward peace.

—Charlie Dawes
Pastor of Hill City Church,
Author, *Simple Prayer*

I've often wondered about the Apostle Paul's comment in Philippians 4:11, "I have learned in whatever state I am, to be content." The verb, "learned," is the operative word to me. Contentment does not come naturally. It is a learning experience. Chris Maxwell brings us into this "learning lab" of growing into Christ and His contentment. This book is not a hurried read. This is a book of reading, reflection, pausing, praying, waiting, finding. It's the learning journey of all-sufficient grace that flows from these pages.

—Dr. Doug Beacham
General Superintendent
International Pentecostal Holiness Church

The relentless pursuit of achievement and success often overshadows the more important virtue of ministry and leadership: contentment. I've seen a lack of contentment kill more ministry dreams than moral failures. Thankfully, Chris Maxwell reminds us of the biblical truth that contentment is learned behavior. You can't help but desire contentment as you read this book.

—Doug Clay
General Superintendent
General Council of the Assemblies of God

We proclaim, "I have a need—a need for speed." This need invades every aspect of our lives and every inch of our soul. In the process, the mad dash, the clock-driven life has robbed us of one of God's greatest gifts ... contentment. In its place running rampant is chaos, clutter, and confusion.

Chris Maxwell goes to battle for us and digs out the forgotten or overlooked distinctives, benefits, and necessity of developing real, storm-weathering, sickness-facing, and victories-won contentment that can only be found and rooted in Christ. No gimmicks are offered here. No quick fixes. Just tried-and-true practices that have to be worked into the fabric of our lives and the moments of our calendars until they impact how we think and live. Carefully read and applied, this book can become a playbook to regain the attitude of Christ so that we too can say, and even more importantly mean, "Nevertheless, Your will, not mine, be done!"

—Steve Ely
Director of Clergy Development
International Pentecostal Holiness Church

Chris Maxwell has given us more than a book—he's given us a roadmap for the journey. Chris does more than write about godly principles—he lives them.

—Hal Donaldson
President/CEO
Convoy of Hope

I think my friend Chris Maxwell knows me better than I realized. He seems, through what he's written in this engaging book, to recognize what ails me. He sees clearly what sometimes drags down my soul. Perhaps I should say our souls. "The most personal is the most universal" the adage goes. What Chris has found in his own struggles became, he writes, "a whispered gift." A revelation for him, yes, as he recounts so well in these pages. But an inspiring, enduring gift for me, too, and, I'm sure, for lots of us.

—Timothy Jones
Pastor,
Author, *Fully Beloved:*
Meeting God in Our Heartaches and Our Hopes

I know many people who are too busy or too tired to read this book because they are scurrying on the proverbial hamster wheel, on an endless search for more significance, more possessions or more fame. This book offers all of us a reset. Chris Maxwell invites us to unplug, declutter, and unwind. He reminds us to build a holy rhythm in our lives, a rhythm that can only be found in the peaceful security of God's unconditional love and approval. This book will be like therapy for some people, like medicine for others and like a cup of cold water for many. I pray we will all trade our frazzled anxiety for Christ's contentment.

—J. Lee Grady
Director, The Mordecai Project
Author, *Set My Heart on Fire* and *Lead Like Paul*

We've become a culture of goal-setters, dream-chasers, and purpose-finders. All of which have their place. But if you lack contentment where you are, or with who you are, running after the next great thing will not satisfy. Chris Maxwell addresses this modern-day dilemma with a book about the value of contentment that's biblical, practical, and oh so relevant.

—Karl Vaters
Author,
Founder of Helping Small Churches Thrive, *KarlVaters.com*

Bookstore shelves are filled with titles promising to show us how to make more money, make more friends, rise higher in our profession, grow a bigger church. We're continually urged to acquire more, achieve more, become more. In his latest book, Chris Maxwell shows us a "more excellent way," the way of contentment.

But is it really possible to find contentment in this world, in your life? There's an easy way to find out. Turn off the clamoring voices around you and the competitive voice inside you. Listen to Chris's calm voice of wisdom and experience. Try out his practical suggestions. You just may discover that contentment really is within your reach, once you know where to look.

—Russell Board, author
Regional Director for Continental Asia
IPHC World Missions Ministries

In my thirty-five years in the counseling field, I have worked with clients searching for contentment, yet finding it to be not only elusive but seemingly impossible. Chris Maxwell's wisdom, insight and candor throughout his work make this elusive state of contentment obtainable. These discontented clients are often depressed about the past and anxious about the future because they do not know how to be content in the present. Chris Maxwell takes the mystery away about how to achieve this desired state. Through painful vulnerability, self-disclosure, wisdom from Scripture, and many practical exercises, Chris provides not just the path to contentment, but tools to remain there on a daily basis. I highly recommend this work to all in search of better mental, emotional, and spiritual health. This book is one that you will want to keep and read again and again.

—Monte Drenner
LPC, MCAP

I met Chris over forty years ago, maybe seven months after first becoming a Christian. Since then, partly due to my vocation and partly due to my inclinations, I've read quite a bit of theology from the church fathers to the present and from multiple Christian traditions. But Chris's book, written as it is in elegant but straightforward language, changed my life and thinking in ways like nothing I've read has in many years. I've always struggled with the idea of contentment. I felt like it implied accepting the unacceptable in my life and, more than that, it meant apathy, and that is not the person I am. Chris brought me around to a more biblical view of contentment that's applicable to my own life and thinking in the here and now: contentment is satisfaction in God and with God regardless of one's circumstances. In fact, I now see that contentment gives me the resilience to change my life and confront my circumstances while remaining in God's peace. My mind and feelings haven't fully changed, but I already see a difference and I feel I am moving in a better direction now. I think you may feel the same way after reading this book.

—Dr. James Rovira
author

Contentment is not a status to attain or a goal to achieve. Rather, contentment is a grace to receive and practice to embrace. In our culture, contentment is a precious, rare commodity dependent on favorable circumstances mostly beyond our control and almost always beyond our reach. Biblical, Christ-centered contentment is offered to us through a vital relationship with God the Father through Jesus the Son supplied by the Holy Spirit.

As I have read and reread the manuscript of Chris' newest book, I have been inspired, informed, and influenced to recognize that contentment is within our grasp. Even mine. Like Chris's counselor, I have a front-row seat into the life and times of Chris Maxwell as we communicate almost every day about our lives at a deeply meaningful level. I have seen Chris learning and leaning into this life of contentment and experienced many of the results alongside him. This is not a concept to be learned. It is a lifestyle to live. And it is accessible if your heart so desires.

I encourage anyone and everyone to read the words, follow the suggestions, experiment with the practices, and find yourself surrounded by a whole new realm of joy, peace, love, gratitude, and contentment. This book can help you. I know because it is helping me.

—Dr. C. Tracy Reynolds
Campus Pastor, Grace Fellowship Madison
Co-host with Chris Maxwell of Next Step Leadership Podcast

Pastor and spiritual director Chris Maxwell offers us an invitation toward clarity and purpose in Contentment: What You Are Searching for Is Already Yours. Chris reminds us that contentment is not giving up or living in passivity—it is learning to live with life-giving intention, which leads to freedom and abundance in all the good ways. If you desire to stop the chase and embrace the goodness of God and the path of fruitfulness in the Christian life, look no further. Chris is a wonderful guide because he lives what he teaches and walks with us through his pastoral and practical words. This is going to be a go-to read on my bookshelf for years to come.

—Seana Scott
Writer, Founder of Well Soul Life

Chris Maxwell's unique writing style has produced a valuable resource, a book titled Contentment. The statements and questions throughout the book strike a good balance for the reader, prompting personal reflection. Chris Maxwell helps us understand that contentment is not about reaching a destination, but encourages the reader to discover ourselves. Chris's comments, observations, and conclusions about the subject of contentment offer a clear understanding of what contentment is not, what it is, and how we can cultivate a life of contentment. Taking the time to read this book will benefit the reader and serve as an excellent tool for sharing with others.

—Bishop Tim Lamb
LifePoint Ministries IPHC
Conference Superintendent

What can set us free from the relentless craving that permeates our consumer-driven world? Writing as a wise sage, Chris Maxwell answers this question by issuing an invitation to receive God's gracious gift of contentment. He skillfully and gently guides the reader down a path toward the freedom, joy, and rest that comes from a life set free from hustle, comparison, and competition. I encourage you to read this engaging book. In doing so, you will discover the deep joy that resonates within the sacred rhythms of a contented life.

—Cheryl Bridges Johns, Ph.D.
Distinguished Visiting Professor & Director,
Pentecostal House of Study
United Theological Seminary

DISCOVER MORE CONTENMENT

This book includes access to additional resources including video teaching, audio, workshops, and community!

Just click on the Access Code below to discover how the book in your hands can become a portal to a new discovery experience!

Contentment

What You're Searching for Is Already Yours

Chris Maxwell

Contentment: What You're Searching for Is Already Yours

by Chris Maxwell

True Potential, Inc

ISBN Print: 9781971560021

ISBN eBook: 9781971560038

True Potential, Inc.
PO Box 904, Travelers Rest, SC 29690
www.truepotentialmedia.com

Printed in the United States of America.

THANK YOU

I want to offer a huge thank you to the people—the many people—who have helped me learn about contentment and who continue helping me live it.

To the unknown and unnoticed ones who serve quietly with a calmness and peace so often missing in my world and in our world.

To the writers whose words taught me what contentment can be and how I might live with more of it.

To my counselor, Monte Drenner, for allowing me to include the story of that day when you spoke the word *contentment* into my life.

To other counselors, pastors, mentors, accountability partners, church members, friends, and even strangers who have displayed contentment in their own unique ways—I'm still learning from so many of you.

To my family, who has been patient and content with me even when I've not lived contentment well—thank you. I'm deeply grateful for each of you.

To my editors—James Rovira, Ann Byle, and Paul Smith—thank you for helping my reflections and confessions become readable material for a wider audience.

To my publisher, Steve Spillman, for being content to work with someone like me—thank you for believing in this message.

And to you, the reader—thank you for opening this book and opening your heart. I pray that through these words you might catch a glimpse of the quiet, beautiful environment of contentment.

May we all find a home there.

CONTENTS

INTRODUCTION THE SEARCH THAT NEVER HAD TO BEGIN

> *Here's the deal: A lack of contentment leaves you chasing—always chasing—the next big thing you hope will make you happy. It's exhausting! You may run in one direction and then another, but you'll always come up short and out of breath.* **—Rachel Cruz**[1]

Our time was almost over. A December visit with my counselor in the northeast Georgia mountains felt right—a final dialogue before another year concluded.

My coat over the chair behind me. His coffee cooling beside my water on the table. Our voices calm but serious. The window framing mountains like watchful companions. The conversation encouraged, challenged, confirmed, inspired.

And then something changed.
With only a few minutes left, he said, "I have one word I want you to think about before you leave. It might be a word for you to process as you end this year and begin the next."

1 Rachel Cruze, *The Contentment Journal*, "Part 3: Contentment" (Mahwah, NJ: Ramsey Press, 2019).

I grabbed my phone to write down the word—the one word.

I didn't want to forget the word—the one word.

After a pause he said, "Contentment."

I didn't expect that word. I hadn't even guessed what it might be. But I typed it quickly. And processed it slowly. The one word landed like a whispered gift—an unexpected dessert at the end of a delicious meal.

When I didn't respond, my counselor asked, "Are you okay with that word?"

Staring out the window, then glancing back at my phone, I said yes. Not with words. With a nod. As I thought and processed and reflected on the word. Later I did say yes with words—many words—words about his word to me.

I knew in that moment *contentment* was more than a counselor's idea.

It was the mindset I needed then. I still need it now.

I ended that December and began the new year journaling, reading, praying, studying, processing, and trying to understand what contentment really meant. What had others learned about it? What did I need to learn? Why did the counselor think contentment was the word for me? When the counselor spoke that word, why did I know so deeply that contentment was the word, the right word, for me?

I wanted to learn about it. I want to understand it. And I wanted to live it.

I'm still trying to learn it, to understand it, to live it.

How? By sharing this journey with you. The questions, the clashes, the prayers, the mistakes, the small victories. Writing my thoughts helps me pursue contentment.

I hope reading my thoughts will help you.

That word—contentment—has stayed with me since I wrote it on my iPhone while listening to my counselor.

I didn't want to just study it. I wanted to live it.

This book is the chronicle of that quest. Not a search for something far away, but for something that's already here. Something many of us overlook. Something I hope you'll discover—maybe for the first time—as you read these pages.

But be aware of this: There's a lie that's louder than ever. It says you're not enough. Not productive enough. Not wealthy enough. Not smart enough. Not noticed enough.

So you scroll. You compare. You perform. You try harder.

And still, something feels missing.

I know that feeling well. I've lived it—while pastoring small churches, writing books that never made bestseller lists, and paying for medical procedures I didn't plan for. I've watched an illness interrupt my rhythm and brain damage try to write the narrative for me. I've felt like less. Less than I hoped to be. Less than others appeared to be. The lie seemed way too true.

I've cared for people and prayed for people and listened to people. Their own scars hurt my heart. Their own stories impacted mine. Contentment too often felt too far away.

But somewhere along the way, I discovered—and I continue discovering—something deeper than all that noise. Something steadier than applause. Something stronger than shame. Something called contentment.

Not the lazy kind. Not the give-up kind. Not the pretend-everything's-fine kind.

But the real kind. The sacred kind.

The kind that breathes peace into our hurried, hurting lives.

This book is a collection of confessions about my investigation and application of the word *contentment*. It is also an invitation. Not to settle—but to see. Not to withdraw—but to wait well. Not to avoid—but to abide.

CONTENTMENT

You don't have to chase more. You don't have to prove anything. You don't have to become someone else to be okay.

There is fulfillment available right here, in your real life, even if the world says otherwise.

This is a quiet rebellion. A different way to live.

Contentment isn't something you achieve. It's something you allow. Like an unexpected treat at the end of a hard conversation—receive it. Let it nourish your soul.

SECTION ONE
RETHINKING CONTENTMENT

1 THE QUIET POWER OF ENOUGH

> *"God is enough. And I have God. Therefore, I have all I need."*
> **—Alyssa Joy Bethke**[2]

We are seekers. We chase, strive, scroll, compare, hustle. We reach for what's just ahead, just out of reach—thinking maybe this next thing will quiet the ache inside. But what if the very thing we're chasing has been quietly present all along?

What if the quiet power of enough—that missing element of contentment—is possible?

Not as denial. Not as settling. But as a steady way of seeing, a grounded way of living, a sacred realization that we already hold more than we know.

This book was born in that realization. Not in moments of success, but in seasons of struggle. Not when life was tidy, but when it felt unmanageable and undone. Not when applause echoed, but when silence lingered. Not while working one job with a predicted schedule, but many jobs and many roles on most days and most times.

Through medical challenges, vocational limitations, personal doubts, and cultural noise, I've had to come back—again and again—to the

2 Alyssa Joy Bethke, *Satisfied: Finding Hope, Joy, and Contentment Right Where You Are* (Worthy Books: Encinitas, CA, 2021), 113.

quiet truth that contentment is not earned or found on a mountaintop of accomplishment. It is received. It is chosen. It is practiced.

And it's available now to each of us.

In these pages, I'll tell stories and confess questions and offer ideas. Together we'll wrestle with tension and name the lies that keep us discontent. We'll explore what Scripture teaches us about this deep, quiet joy. And we'll take practical steps to live differently in a world shouting that we're not enough.

Because maybe the question isn't, "Where do I find contentment?" Maybe the question is, "What would change if I believed I already had it?"

This is your invitation.

Not to escape life—but to step fully into it.

To pay attention. To practice gratitude. To serve. To rest. To find beauty in what seems ordinary. To breathe deeply. To live well. To live content.

Contentment isn't a synonym for laziness.

It isn't avoiding hard conversations or neglecting what matters. It isn't a pretty mask for passivity or a poetic form of escapism.

It is a perspective. A lens to look through. A filter to help us see clearly again.

It's the steady conviction that this life—whatever it looks like right now—is still worth living well. It's the deep breath in the middle of disappointment. It's the silent yes to grace when life doesn't go according to plan. It's the ability to say, "This is enough for now. And I am enough for this."

We live in a world that constantly feeds discontent. Ads, algorithms, and even our own inner voices say, "You should have more. You should be more. You should do more."

But what if the invitation of contentment is something altogether different? What if it's not about shrinking your dreams—but about grounding them? Not about silencing ambition—but about sanctifying it?

What if contentment is where true power begins?

I've watched churches remain small but faithful. I've watched teams lose the game but win in character. I've watched people face surgeries and setbacks and still endure with joy. I've watched others, and I've lived it myself.

The numbers don't always look impressive. The platform doesn't always grow. The results don't always shine.

But the peace? The fulfillment? The grace?

It's real. It's enough.

It's contentment.

This chapter begins your journey. A journey not toward passivity—but toward presence. Not toward less meaning—but toward deeper meaning.

Let's stop chasing what was never meant to satisfy.

Let's start finding fulfillment right here, right now, in the sacred soil of our real lives.

Even if the world says you're not enough, contentment says otherwise.

But why are so many people living without contentment? Why is that the norm? What does a life without contentment become?

Many people equate productivity and success with contentment, believing that if they achieve more, accumulate more, or work harder, they will finally feel fulfilled. This pursuit often backfires because of:

1. **Misplaced Identity:** They tie their worth to their achievements instead of their identity in Christ.
2. **Cultural Pressure:** Society glorifies busyness and accomplishment, making rest and contentment seem countercultural or lazy.

3. **Shifting Goals:** Once a goal is achieved new desires arise, leading to an endless cycle of striving.
4. **The Fear of Failure:** People overwork to avoid inadequacy or rejection, driven by fear rather than purpose.
5. **The Lack of Internal Peace:** Without grounding in God's peace, even hard work can feel empty.

Signs of Discontented Living

1. **Chronic Complaining:** Frequently expressing dissatisfaction about circumstances, possessions, or relationships.
2. **Constant Comparison:** Comparison to others, leading to feelings of inadequacy or envy.
3. **Restlessness:** Always seeking the next achievement, possession, or milestone, believing it will bring happiness.
4. **Materialism:** Placing excessive value on acquiring possessions or wealth but feeling empty after obtaining them.
5. **Discontent with Current Circumstances:** Wishing life was different instead of accepting and finding joy in the present.
6. **Difficulty Enjoying the Present:** Being overly focused on "what's next" or "what could be" instead of savoring current moments.
7. **Jealousy or Envy:** Feeling bitter or resentful toward others who appear to have more or better things.
8. **Workaholism:** Overworking to prove oneself or find fulfillment, often at the expense of health or relationships.
9. **Anxiety About the Future:** Worrying excessively about money, status, or success.
10. **Frequent Regret or Bitterness:** Dwelling on past mistakes or lost opportunities instead of embracing the present.

None of those are preferred life goals. None of those are what we wake up in the morning to pursue.

So why are we so often trapped in a cave of discontent? Why is contentment an elusive art?

I was reminded one night.

It was late. The noise of life finally quieted enough for me to hear myself think. Yet, in the silence, I felt the tension. A war raged within—desires unmet, goals unfinished, and comparisons that whispered accusations. The world has taught us to keep striving, to demand more, to never settle. But Jesus offers us a countercultural invitation: contentment.

My mind stayed there. Thinking about Jesus. Thinking about the contentment He seeks to bring into my hurry and worry. Thinking about what contentment is and what it is not.

Contentment isn't laziness or mediocrity. It's a quiet confidence that who we are, where we are, and what we have is enough because God is enough.

Contentment frees us from the endless chase and anchors us in God's sufficiency. It replaces anxiety with peace, greed with gratitude, and dissatisfaction with joy.

Jesus modeled contentment in ways that feel foreign to our culture. He didn't own land, build an empire, or measure His worth by earthly success. Instead, He trusted His Father fully, lived simply, and gave generously. When He taught His disciples to pray, "Give us this day our daily bread," He was inviting them into a life of trusting God for enough. His life reminds us that contentment isn't found in possessions or achievements—it's found in relationship with God.

We resist contentment because the world tells us we're not enough. Social media feeds this lie with curated perfection, always hinting that we need more to be happy. Advertisers convince us to buy, upgrade, and consume. Past mistakes haunt us, whispering that we need to do more to prove our worth. Future fears nudge us toward hoarding resources, just in case.

Even in ministry, contentment feels elusive. Pastors struggle with comparison, burnout, and unmet expectations. The church down the street seems to grow faster, their sermons trend online, their budgets overflow. It's easy to forget that ministry isn't about performance—it's about faithfulness.

As I reflect, I confess my own discontentment. I've chased applause instead of resting in God's approval. I've envied others' successes, forgetting the sacredness of my own journey. I've failed to notice the miracles of the ordinary—the warmth of a friendship, the sunrise after a hard night, the quiet assurance of God's presence.

But contentment isn't a destination; it's a discipline, a lifestyle, a journey. It is an adventure you are invited to join—into the quiet power of enough.

2
WHAT CONTENTMENT IS NOT

> *"Discontent is an anxious state of mind, which dries the brains, wastes the spirits, and corrodes and eats away the comfort of life."*
> **—Thomas Watson**[3]

Ever felt the pull to give up—not because you've found peace but because you're just tired?

The unopened emails stacking up your inbox. The dishes in the sink you can't bring yourself to wash. The meeting you're supposed to lead, but you're running on fumes.

Or maybe it's deeper. The dream that didn't work out. The prayers that feel unanswered. The quiet thought: *Why keep trying at all?*

You can confuse contentment with quitting. We can think "enough" means we've stopped caring. We can wonder if slowing down is the same as giving up.

It's not neglect. It's not escape. It isn't code for slacking off or checking out. It isn't an excuse to quit dreaming or stop showing up.

Contentment doesn't equal avoiding important issues or neglecting vital tasks. It doesn't dismiss injustice. It doesn't downplay urgency. It

3 Thomas Watson, *The Art of Divine Contentment: In Modern English*, translation and annotations by Jason Roth (Oswego, IL: Godlipress, 2017), 39.

doesn't mean we no longer care. Some people pretend they've reached a state of peace when, in reality, they've just built emotional bunkers. They label themselves "content" while quietly giving up.

But that's not real contentment. That's fear dressed up in calming language.

Contentment shouldn't become a preferred method of escapism.

It isn't apathy. It is alignment.

It's not a way to run from pain or pretending life doesn't hurt. It's not a mask we wear so others won't see the disappointment behind our eyes.

We don't find peace by ignoring our reality. We find it by facing it—and choosing a better response than panic, envy, or shame.

True contentment doesn't deny the difficulty. It simply refuses to let the difficulty decide everything.

Without true contentment we put ourselves in difficult positions.

How can we be sure of what contentment is not?

Not Passivity

Don't confuse rest with escaping. Don't confuse peace with passivity. People who live with deep contentment still care. They still take action. They still pray, speak up, show up, work hard, and make change. But they do all of it from a posture that says, "God really is enough. What God does in me and through me really is enough. I don't need to prove anything to myself or anyone else."

They're not trying to earn love or prove their worth. They've already received it.

Not Settling for Less

Some say, "I guess I should just be content," as if that means giving up hope. But contentment isn't hopelessness. It isn't surrendering your dreams or desires. It's holding your hope without it owning you. It's loving your life—even when it doesn't give you everything you want.

Negative Side Effects of Living Without Contentment

1. **Mental and Emotional Stress:** Chronic dissatisfaction can lead to anxiety, depression, and a lack of inner peace.
2. **Strained Relationships:** Envy, comparison, or prioritizing possessions over people can damage relationships.
3. **Physical Health Problems:** Stress and unhappiness may contribute to high blood pressure, heart disease, and a weakened immune system.
4. **Burnout:** Constant striving for more can lead to physical and emotional exhaustion.
5. **Financial Problems:** Pursuing materialism or living beyond one's means can result in debt and financial stress.
6. **Lack of Gratitude:** Focusing on what's lacking diminishes appreciation for blessings, which impacts emotional well-being.
7. **Chronic Dissatisfaction:** A constant sense of "not enough" leads to unhappiness regardless of achievements or possessions.
8. **Erosion of Faith:** A discontented heart can struggle to trust God's provision and plan, leading to spiritual distance.
9. **Missed Joy in the Present:** Focusing on "what's next" or "what's wrong" prevents people from fully enjoying their current blessings.
10. **Increased Risk of Addiction:** Seeking escape through substances, shopping, or other addictive behaviors to fill the void left by discontentment.

It's saying, "I'll still believe. I'll still work. But I won't let the unfinished parts keep me from peace today."

Not Indifference

Content people are not indifferent. They feel deeply. They grieve. They wrestle. They care. They pray bold prayers. They carry heavy burdens.

But they have also learned how to breathe when the weight won't lift. They've learned how to trust, even in the tension.

They're not immune to struggle. They've just discovered how to live well within it.

So we name the imposters. We call them what they are.

And we keep walking toward the real thing.

Contentment is needed; it's like a restlessness within us. Not the quick fix. Not the polished version. But the honest, grounded, peace-rooted kind of contentment that stands tall even when the wind keeps blowing.

We live in a world that tells us to reach, climb, strive.

More. Better. Faster. The noise of discontentment is deafening, and our hearts grow weary from trying to keep up. But what if the answer isn't found in the next achievement or possession? What if the ache we feel isn't a call to do more, but to be more present?

Jesus saw this need in the crowds who followed Him, longing for something they couldn't define. To them He said, *"Come to me, all you who are weary and burdened, and I will give you rest"* (Matthew 11:28).

We need that rest today. We need contentment—not as an escape from life's demands, but as a reminder that our souls are not designed to live in constant striving.

Contentment isn't something we earn. It's a gift wrapped in grace and delivered to our hearts when we lean into God's presence.

Paul, writing from a prison cell, spoke of this mystery: "I have learned to be content whatever the circumstances" (Philippians 4:11). How could he say that? Because he knew the Source. Contentment isn't found in the "what"—it's found in the "Who."

I've seen this truth unfold in my own life. There were moments when I felt everything I'd known had been taken away—my health, my plans, my sense of control. And yet, in the stillness of those moments, I discovered that God's peace isn't tied to my circumstances. It is tied to His presence, always available and always enough.

Contentment is a paradox, isn't it? It tiptoes into our lives when we least expect it, or perhaps when we've planned for its arrival. We schedule time to rest and feel its gentle embrace, but then it surprises us in the chaos of unplanned interruptions. Contentment knows no formula—it's not something we calculate or control. Instead, it's a gift we receive, a practice we nurture, a presence we acknowledge.

It comes with sound and silence. The laughter of children, the paragraphs on pages, the conversations with a true friend, the melody of a favorite song, the evening breeze on a cool autumn day—these can awaken our awareness of life's goodness. Contentment might arrive in the stillness, when the noise fades and we hear only the rhythm of our own breathing. Can we learn to appreciate both? To treasure the music of community and the quiet of solitude?

Contentment finds us inside and outside. Indoors in the familiar corners of our homes, where memories are woven into the fabric of the furniture. Outdoors where the sky stretches wide, reminding us of God's vastness. It's in the living room with family and on the trail alone, inhaling creation's perfume. It's not bound by location but by perspective—learning to see God's beauty everywhere.

It appears at the beginning of a task when the potential feels fresh and the possibilities endless. And it lingers at the end when the work is done, the mess cleared, the goal reached. But contentment also shows up somewhere in the messy middle when progress feels slow and the finish line far away. Can we find joy in the process, not just the result?

Contentment whispers to us when we're energetic and when we're exhausted. In the buzz of productivity, it reminds us to pause and appreciate the moment. In the weariness of fatigue, it invites us to rest and trust that we are enough—even when we feel like we've done nothing at all.

It meets us in a crowd when we're surrounded by friends or strangers, part of something larger than ourselves. It also finds us when we're alone, when the quiet stretches long and we are left with only our thoughts and God's presence.

Contentment doesn't require perfect faith. It's there when we're full of confidence and sure of God's goodness. And it doesn't flee when doubt clouds our vision. Even when questions arise, when faith feels fragile, contentment remains—a quiet reassurance that God holds us in every season.

It comes in celebration, when joy overflows and we can't stop smiling. And it comes in grief, when tears fall freely and hearts feel heavy. In both, contentment isn't a dismissal of emotions but an acknowledgment that God is present in all of it.

Good quotes, life principles, and even Scripture can cause us to misunderstand or misplace true contentment. Popular trends offer what we think might bring contentment, but they do not.

When misapplied, even well-intentioned guidance can lead to discontentment:

1. **Pursuing Big Dreams:** Focusing solely on the dream can overshadow God's timing and cause frustration when progress feels slow.
2. **Having Huge Faith:** Comparing our faith to others' outward faith can lead to feelings of inadequacy.
3. **Working Hard:** Overworking without rest can make us idolize achievement rather than relying on God.
4. **Taking Risks:** When risks fail, discouragement can set in if our identity is tied to success.
5. **Believing in the Big:** Focusing on "big" goals might make us overlook the beauty of small, everyday moments.
6. **Enduring:** Persevering without joy or gratitude can lead to bitterness or burnout.
7. **Internal Peace:** Seeking peace without surrendering control to God can turn it into just another unattainable goal.

Even Scripture and spiritual principles can become burdens when we approach them legalistically, turning them into tasks rather than invitations to rely on God.

Living without true contentment robs people of peace, joy, and connection with others. It creates a cycle of striving and dissatisfaction that ultimately harms mental, emotional, and physical health. Recognizing the signs and cultivating contentment can lead to a more fulfilling and balanced life.

We live in a world of extremes. Chase more. Or chase nothing. Work endlessly. Or check out completely. Demand significance. Or disengage from purpose. Contentment doesn't live in those extremes. It walks a different road. A slower one. A steady one. And it starts by naming the counterfeits.

Because if we misunderstand what contentment isn't, we'll never discover what it actually is.

Maybe contentment isn't something we find, but something that finds us. When we open our hearts to both the planned and the unexpected, the loud and the quiet, the joy and the sorrow—contentment weaves its way into our lives. It's a reminder that God is with us. Not just on the mountaintops or in the valleys, but with every ordinary step in between.

So today, whether you're beginning or ending, alone or surrounded, strong or weary, may you pause long enough to notice that contentment is here.

Right here. Right now.

Waiting for you to see it, to receive it, to live it.

3 WHAT CONTENTMENT IS

Christian contentment is a heart work, deep and interior.
—Andrew W. Davis[4]

Contentment is a perspective for life.

A lens to see through. A view of great value. A life commitment.

Contentment is not found on sale or discovered on vacation. It's not a fleeting emotion or a weekend retreat. It's not a tentative pleasure or a game-winning hit. It's something deeper—something formed over time, something chosen again and again.

It's a different way of looking at the same life.

It is the inner "enough."

Not because everything is easy or what we have feels like enough, but because something within us is becoming settled.

Remember what Paul wrote from a prison cell? Not from a resort. Not after a bonus. But surrounded by the stench and strain of suffering. Hear the echo of his heart: *"I have learned to be content whatever the circumstances."* (Philippians 4:11).

4 Andrew W. Davis, *The Power of Christian Contentment: Finding Deeper, Richer, Christ-Centered Joy* (Grand Rapids, MI: Baker Books, 2019), 43.

Learned.

Not downloaded. Not inherited. Not instantly available.

Learned.

Through losses, through victories, through seasons of silence, through the tension of waiting.

Contentment is not giving up; it's standing firm.

It's refusing to live life as if you're always behind. It's resisting the script that says you're not doing enough, being enough, earning enough, posting enough. It's rewriting that script—daily, regularly—with words like grace, rest, equilibrium, presence, and peace.

Contentment is breathing—right where you are.

Not someday. Not when things finally change.

But now.

In this room. With these people. In this story. At this time.

It's being fully awake to the moment you've been given, without needing to escape into some idealized future version.

Contentment is courageous.

It's not soft. It's not weak.

It's brave because it dares to love what is. It dares to let go of the illusions and live fully in the real.

It wakes up each morning and says, "This life is still worth living, even here."

Even now. Still worth living.

When you hold contentment, you don't have to hold control. Or attempt that impossible exertion of seeking control.

You can release. You can rest. You can trust. You can live as one who is free.

Let's not chase contentment as a product. Let's cultivate it as a posture.

Let's not wait for it to arrive. Let's learn to live it now.

Let's see it for what it really is: A gift. A guide. A quiet rebellion.

Content—Even Here?

Can I be content with the way I'm wired?

With the parts of me that feel different—unique—maybe even inconvenient to others?

Can I grow where I need to grow, while also choosing to accept the pieces of me that won't ever quite fit the mold?

Content—when others are drawn to flashing lights, moving parts, noise, and spectacle, but I quietly step back—knowing those things could trigger seizures?

Content—when a conversation turns chaotic, when everyone talks at once, while I long for calmness and focus and one voice at a time?

Content—when the numbers in the bank account don't add up? When I'm doing my best but still unsure how it will all work out?

Content—when someone asks, "Remember when ...?" And I don't. Not because I don't care, but because my brain just doesn't hold memories the way it used to, the way I wish it would.

Content—when I know I need to work hard, push forward, stretch and strengthen? And also content when I recognize that some things aren't worth the extra striving?

Content—when I keep inviting people closer, but they don't seem as interested in walking the same road with me?

Content—when I need sleep—early nights, slow mornings—while others seem to run endlessly without rest?

Content—when my prayers don't unfold the way I pictured? When the waiting stretches long and the answers don't make sense?

It helps me mentally process by considering words similar to contentment. Glance at this list. Think about each synonym. Think about yourself as you read the definitions:

1. **Satisfaction:** A feeling of being pleased and fulfilled with what you have or have achieved.
2. **Peace:** A calm and tranquil state of mind, free from worry or striving.
3. **Gratitude:** A deep sense of thankfulness and appreciation for the blessings in life.
4. **Fulfillment:** The feeling of completeness or achieving a sense of purpose.
5. **Serenity:** A state of calmness and inner stillness, regardless of external circumstances.
6. **Acceptance:** Embracing life as it is without resistance or longing for something different.
7. **Happiness:** A general sense of well-being and satisfaction with life.
8. **Equanimity:** Mental composure and balance, especially during challenging situations.
9. **Rest:** A state of repose or relief from striving, often linked to spiritual trust in God.
10. **Ease:** A lightness or absence of difficulty in one's approach to life, stemming from contentment.

Each of these terms emphasizes different aspects of contentment but captures the essence of being at peace with oneself and one's circumstances.

Think also about this statement: contentment is possible.

Contentment doesn't just happen—it's something we practice, a daily decision to live differently in a culture of discontentment.

It begins with small steps:

- Pause to notice what you already have.

- Pray for eyes to see the blessings you've overlooked.
- Choose gratitude, even when life feels incomplete.

I remember a day when everything felt heavy—the deadlines, the demands, the doubts. In the middle of it all, I stepped outside and noticed the way the sunlight filtered through the trees. For a moment, I let myself simply be. That moment didn't change my circumstances, but it changed me.

Contentment is possible when we practice seeing the world with God's perspective, one moment at a time.

Contentment is also healing. It brings peace that restores us.

Discontentment wounds us. It fractures our relationships, fuels our anxieties, and blinds us to the good in front of us. But contentment? Contentment heals.

When we embrace contentment, we find peace where there was once striving. We find joy where there was once comparison. We find rest where there was once exhaustion.

One day I sat with a friend who was dying of cancer. He smiled as he spoke of how much time he probably had left. Did you read what I wrote? He smiled. Not with despair. With gratitude. "I've learned to treasure what I have," he said. "I've stopped asking why and started saying thank you."

His words stayed with me. He lived with peace. Contentment doesn't mean avoiding pain—it means finding God's goodness within it. It's a balm for the soul, reminding us that even in our brokenness, we are held by a God who makes all things new. It is peace arriving when often least expected.

Peace: More Than a Feeling

Peace isn't just a side effect of contentment—it's a companion, a fruit, a promise, and a Person. When Scripture speaks of peace, it doesn't refer only to the absence of conflict or the soothing of emotions. It speaks of *shalom*—wholeness, harmony, restoration of things to how they were meant to be. That's why peace is not something we manufacture; it's something we receive.

Jesus is called the Prince of Peace (Isaiah 9:6). Before His death, He told His disciples, "Peace I leave with you; my peace I give you. I do not give to you as the world gives" (John 14:27). The peace Jesus gives isn't dependent on outward comfort. It doesn't disappear in chaos or dissolve in heartache. It remains, even in storms. It stays, even as the number of days remaining in life run short.

Peace is also a fruit of the Spirit (Galatians 5:22). It grows as we stay rooted in God, as we surrender outcomes, and as we embrace presence over pressure. We lose God's peace when we strive for control, when we fill our minds with fear, or when we compare ourselves with others. But we can return to peace through prayer, stillness, Scripture, deep breathing, and worship.

Peace is not passive. It's not pretending everything is fine. It's actively trusting that God is with us even when everything is not fine. It's making a choice—sometimes daily, sometimes hourly—to return our minds to Christ, who calms our internal chaos with His word and presence.

Here are a few practical ways to embrace peace:

- Start your day by breathing deeply and repeating a promise of peace (e.g., John 14:27 or Philippians 4:7).
- Create "peace pauses" throughout your day—moments of stillness, silence, or prayer.
- Limit the noise: social media, news, and hurry can all rob you of peace.
- Memorize and reflect on Scripture passages about peace.
- Ask God to help you recognize what's stealing your peace—and give you courage to set boundaries or shift focus.

Ultimately, peace is not a reward for figuring everything out. It's a gift offered by God. It's not always a feeling—it's a reality we can choose to step into, no matter our circumstances.

And that is the perspective we should contemplate. Whatever is waiting to be seen, including peace, our perception changes through the lens of contentment.

4

THE COMPARISON TRAP

Reaching my goal didn't make me happy. **—Heather Creekmore**[5]

One of our grandchildren was sick, so I told him he couldn't get too close to me. No hugs. No high-fives. Just smiles from a safe distance.

"Why?" he asked.

Before I could answer, he said, "I like close."

I do too. I think we all do—deep down. Close friends. Close families. Close communities. Close moments. Close relationships. Close together.

But too many people keep too much distance. Maybe because the last time we got close, we got hurt. So we live detached, convinced it's safer that way.

Let's change that.

Let's choose close.

Let's like close.

---

5 Heather Creekmore, *The Comparison-Free Life: How to Stop Comparing & Find Joy, Peace, and Rest* (Abilene, TX: Leafwood Publishers, 2024).

Because contentment often grows in closeness—not in isolation. Not in distance. But in relationships where love has room to breathe.

Too often, instead of leaning into closeness, we chase something else.

The newer. The more expensive. The more colorful. The more admired.

The higher-ranked team. The louder song. The fancier car. The house with a view.

That restaurant instead of the other one. That clothing brand instead of the one on sale. A more polished speaker, preacher, singer, or strategist. A trending voice in culture. A constantly growing following.

First place or fifth place—or left out completely. Stat sheets and shoes worn by stars. Slogans and sales numbers.

What do they have in common?

They're comparisons. Status measured on the surface. Value interpreted by popularity, performance, and platform.

You hear it in the sigh when your friend mentions the raise she just got. You see it in the forced smile when the couple across the table announces their engagement. You notice it in the late-night scrolling—thumb pausing over vacation photos that look happier than your reality. You catch it in the silence after someone brags about their child's scholarship, while another parent quietly stirs her coffee. You feel it in yourself when a neighbor steers a new car into the driveway, headlights sweeping across your old one.

In that world, contentment doesn't stand a chance. It is drowned in the noise of comparison. It's shoved in the corner while applause is given to someone else. In that world, enough is never enough.

We should ask biblical characters such as Cain and Abel, or Saul and David, or Christ's first disciples to offer their stories. Or famous stars. Or politicians.

Or me.

Or you.

We know the feeling, don't we? The glance sideways. The scroll through someone else's life. The subtle sigh when their success reminds us of what we lack. A win for them starts to feel like a loss for us.

Comparison is the thief of not only joy—but contentment too.

It starts quietly.

A glance. A scroll. A conversation. A question: Why not me?

We were content—until we weren't. Until someone else got the opportunity. Until their numbers grew and ours didn't. Until their name was mentioned and ours was forgotten.

Comparison doesn't knock politely. It sneaks in, rewrites the story, and steals the peace we had only moments before.

And if we aren't careful, we let it stay.

We feed it. We nurture it. We listen to its whispers: "You should be further along." "You should be more like them." "You're missing out."

But contentment has a different voice.

A kinder one.

It reminds us, "You're not called to their story. You're called to yours."

A Different Scoreboard

Church leaders, business owners, teachers, students, creators—we all have our scoreboards. Attendance. Influence. Sales. Reach. We stare at the numbers, hoping they validate us.

But contentment calls us away from that fixation.

It asks, "What if success isn't size?" "What if meaning isn't measured that way?"

I've had to relearn that lesson again and again.

And yet—contentment rises.

If I let it.

Comparison wants us to hustle. Contentment invites us to rest. Comparison says we're behind. Contentment says we're becoming. Comparison makes life a competition. Contentment makes life a calling.

What If We Let Go?

What if we looked at someone else's success without turning it into our failure? What if we cheered instead of compared? What if we let go of trying to outpace and outshine—and just lived?

Jesus never said, "Follow me ... and look over your shoulder while doing it."

He said, "Follow me." Period.

He said, "Follow me. And I will make you fishers of men." Not, "Follow me and I expect you to impress everyone who is watching."

If you're old enough, you may remember the first time you saw a computer sort data faster than a group of people could process it? What amazed us then has now become expected.

We live in a world of algorithms and automation. Systems execute complex tasks with minimal human input. Words are no longer just spoken; they are transformed into text, images, and audio in seconds. Machines extract insights from datasets. Programs sort and predict and project. Innovation keeps advancing in the fast lane. Faster than our minds can rest. Faster than our souls can breathe.

What we now rely on is breathtaking and overwhelming, convenient and reliable, assisting us and spoiling us.

Technology offers us gifts. But it also tempts us with illusions: newer is always better, faster is always right, bigger is always necessary. We begin measuring our worth by how quickly we can adapt, how immediately we can respond, how many trends we can notice, how well we can keep up.

But maybe we should consider a question. What if contentment does not arrive through the next update, the next immersive technology, the next leap forward?

And this question. What if contentment is found in pausing long enough to see that even in this season of constant progress, the quiet power of "enough" is still more healing than all the noise of "more?"

I do not want to be controlled by systems, datasets, and trends. I want to live free enough to use technology without being used by it. I want to practice presence, to choose gratitude, to find joy in this ordinary moment—this moment that no algorithm could ever fully replicate.

Contentment doesn't come from climbing higher than others. It comes from walking faithfully where you are. Not trying to live someone else's story or living in the algorithms. But living your story—fully, freely, courageously.

That is where contentment is found.

Envy, Jealousy, and the Theft of Contentment

Envy is the desire for what someone else has.

Jealousy is the fear of losing what we already have—or the resentment when someone else gets what we feel we deserve.

These emotions don't just visit us; they settle in if we let them. And when they do, they distort our view, divide our relationships, and drain our contentment.

Scripture warns us clearly:

"A heart at peace gives life to the body, but envy rots the bones."—Proverbs 14:30

"Love is patient, love is kind. It does not envy."—1 Corinthians 13:4

"You are still worldly. For since there is jealousy and quarreling among you, are you not worldly?"—1 Corinthians 3:3

Envy and jealousy whisper lies:

"You're not enough."

"You deserve more."

"They have what should've been yours."

But contentment tells the truth:

"You are already loved."

"You have what matters most."

"You don't have to compete."

Practical ways to resist envy and jealousy:

- Name it. Admit when envy or jealousy creeps in. Confession brings clarity.
- Celebrate others. Shift your focus from comparison to cheering for them.
- Give thanks. Gratitude is a shield against envy.
- Practice presence. Stay where your feet are. Envy often pulls you into someone else's lane.
- Pray honestly. Tell God how you feel. Ask Him to change your heart.

Contentment grows when we stop looking sideways and start looking upward.

Jesus invites us not to copy each other's lives but to walk faithfully in our own.

Contentment in the Broken Pieces

God doesn't waste our pain. Have you heard that before? Have you read it? What does it mean to you?

What we see as broken, He uses to build something new. Contentment comes when we stop fighting against the cracks in our stories and start finding beauty in how His light shines through them.

When I see scars—the ones I wear on my body and the ones etched in my story—I no longer feel shame. Instead, I feel grace. Healing didn't come the way I expected, but it came, nonetheless. Contentment grew not in the fixing of what was wrong but in trusting that what I had was enough.

Let's learn what contentment isn't.

Let's live what contentment is.

Wave goodbye to comparison. Welcome broken places and grace and trust and peace. Receive contentment, and don't grade yourself on how well you're doing with this plan. Because contentment never needed your perfection—just your willingness.

Why Contentment Seems So Elusive

Jonathan Haidt's *The Anxious Generation* and similar works from contemporary authors and speakers provide valuable insights into why contentment seems so elusive in modern culture. These books and trends reveal how societal shifts, technological advances, and cultural pressures fuel discontentment and anxiety, while offering tools for reflection and growth. Here are some of the key themes and ideas:

1. The Role of Social Media and Comparison

Haidt, alongside authors such as Cal Newport (***Digital Minimalism***) and Johann Hari (***Stolen Focus***), highlights how social media perpetuates comparison and anxiety. Social platforms create a constant feedback loop of curated perfection, leading users to feel "less than" as they scroll through others' highlight reels.

Insights Provided:

- Social media encourages FOMO—a "fear of missing out"—and dissatisfaction with the present moment.
- Validation through likes and comments fosters external approval-seeking rather than internal contentment.

Solutions Offered:

- Practicing digital detoxes or setting screen-time limits.
- Focusing on authentic connections over online validation.

2. Modern Metrics of Success

Haidt and others, such as Brené Brown (***The Gifts of Imperfection***), discuss how modern culture ties worth to achievement, wealth, and productivity. This performance-driven mindset fuels a never-ending quest for "more," making contentment feel unattainable.

Insights Provided:

- The societal push for success often neglects emotional and spiritual health.
- The illusion of control over our lives creates frustration when outcomes don't align with expectations.

Solutions Offered:

- Redefining success to include rest, relationships, and well-being.
- Embracing vulnerability and authenticity as part of the human experience.

3. Anxiety as a Cultural Epidemic

Haidt's analysis of anxiety among younger generations points to cultural and systemic causes, including overprotective parenting, economic uncertainty, and the breakdown of traditional community structures. Books such as Hari's ***Lost Connections*** and ***The Coddling of the American Mind*** (co-written by Haidt) explore these themes.

Insights Provided:

- Rising anxiety stems from a lack of resilience, excessive individualism, and weakened social ties.
- The loss of stable anchors such as faith, family, and community leads to a sense of disorientation.

Solutions Offered:

- Rebuilding connections through community engagement and meaningful relationships.
- Developing coping mechanisms and resilience through mindfulness and gratitude practices.

4. The Influence of Modern Trends on Contentment

Books such as ***The Ruthless Elimination of Hurry*** by John Mark Comer and the minimalist movement (e.g., Marie Kondo's ***The Life-Changing Magic of Tidying Up***) challenge the busyness and materialism of modern life, which undermine contentment.

Insights Provided:

- The pace of life leaves little room for reflection, wonder, or gratitude.
- Materialism feeds a cycle of acquisition but doesn't satisfy deeper needs.

Solutions Offered:

- Prioritizing intentional living by slowing down and simplifying.
- Cultivating gratitude for what we already have instead of striving for what we lack.

5. Rewiring the Mind

Neuroscientists such as Andrew Huberman and popular authors such as Carol Dweck (***Mindset***) emphasize the brain's neuroplasticity—the ability to rewire thoughts and habits. Haidt echoes this idea by suggesting that contentment can be cultivated through deliberate practices.

Insights Provided:

- Our thought patterns are shaped by culture but can be intentionally redirected.

- Practices like meditation, gratitude journaling, and cognitive reframing can combat negative spirals.

Solutions Offered:

- Regularly practicing mindfulness to ground oneself in the present moment.
- Challenging negative beliefs and replacing them with affirmations of God's sufficiency or one's inherent worth.

6. The Return to Ancient Wisdom

Modern culture's dissatisfaction has led many to rediscover ancient spiritual practices. Authors such as Richard Foster (***Celebration of Discipline***) and Henri Nouwen (*The Way of the Heart*) resonate with those seeking deeper contentment by pointing to practices such as prayer, simplicity, and solitude.

Insights Provided:

- Ancient spiritual disciplines offer timeless wisdom for cultivating contentment and peace.
- Contentment grows through a focus on God's provision rather than cultural pressures.

Solutions Offered:

- Embracing silence, fasting, and reflection as part of daily rhythms.
- Finding joy in serving others and aligning life with spiritual values.

INTERLUDE: CHOOSING CONTENTMENT

> *We can be asking for good things with good motivations, but if we've reached the point where the desire for them is making us discontent, we need to make a choice. Do we keep holding onto that desire, or do we daily seek to let it go, so that we can take hold of him and enjoy the contentment he offers?* **—Jennie Pollock**[6]

I used to wait for contentment to find me.

I thought it would arrive when life finally settled, when my circumstances aligned just right. I imagined contentment as a gift that would show up at my door, wrapped in quietness, at ease. But it never did—not like that. Life stayed unpredictable. Circumstances refused to cooperate. And I was left searching.

Then I started noticing something. Contentment didn't come to me; I had to go to it. Not by striving or grasping, but by choosing. By walking toward it, stepping into it, making space for it.

I started waking early, before the world demanded my attention. I sat writing, my prayers stretching onto the pages, my thoughts finding

6 Jennie Pollock, *If Only: Finding Joyful Contentment in the Face of Lack and Longing* (Epsom, Surrey, England: The Good Book Company, 2020), 94.

their place in a journal. I read words—ancient and new—that shaped my soul. I whispered prayers in the dark. I just sat or walked in silence, letting my questions rest in the stillness.

When I walked, it wasn't to get anywhere, but to be there. Step after step, breath after breath, I let the rhythm settle me. I found contentment in the way the trees stood steady, the way the wind whispered through the branches, the way my feet kept moving even when my mind wanted to race ahead.

There were meals alone, meals with family, meals with friends—simple meals, rich with laughter and seasoned with conversation. There were songs with lyrics that made me pause, that helped me pray, that made me think, that reminded me of what is true. There were sports games that let me escape for a while, that pulled me into a story bigger than myself. There were sunrises that called me to gratitude and sunsets that reminded me to rest.

I found contentment in the mountains, where I could breathe deep and remember how small I am. I found it at the ocean where the waves kept coming, steady and sure, like grace. I found it in waterfalls—rushing, relentless, full of movement and mystery. I found it in the stars, in the way they shined without striving, in the way they simply were.

Family moments, lines of poetry, alluring books, worship songs, and quiet contemplation—they all became invitations to contentment. I didn't always take them. Some days I still waited for contentment to come to me. But the best days were the ones I went to it.

I keep choosing. I choose to wake up early when I'd rather sleep in. I choose to walk when I'd rather stay still. I choose to read, pray, write, laugh, listen. I choose to stand in awe of the mountains, to breathe in the ocean air, to watch the sun rise and set.

Contentment is not something we stumble into. It is something we step toward.

So, take a step. Whatever today holds, choose to go where contentment is found. Walk toward it. Wake early. Read. Pray. Write. Laugh. Be with people who remind you what is good. Stand beneath the stars and remember who you are. Listen to a song that stirs your soul. Let yourself be astonished by the beauty around you.

Contentment is waiting. But it won't come to you.

You have to go to it.

Remind yourself what this book is: An Invitation to Contentment

Contentment isn't just a possibility—it's an invitation.

An invitation to rest. To trust. To live fully in the grace of each moment.

Let us accept that invitation today. Let us pause, breathe, and remember that we don't need to have it all to be whole. In Christ, we already have enough.

And in that truth we find the hope, healing, and peace our souls so desperately need.

View unique experiences and challenges as inspiration for creating a life strategy that fosters contentment amid commitments. Here are examples from *my* life of practical steps and reflections which could also become your foundation, that offering relatable wisdom and hope. Read them as examples, then write your own:

1. Be Content Working Five Jobs (I Enjoy Each One).

- View each role you have as a calling, not just work.
- Set boundaries to avoid burnout, ensuring each job gets my full attention during dedicated times.
- Regularly remind myself why I started each role, celebrating the purpose behind the work.
- Delegate when possible and trust others to contribute.
- Write about how juggling multiple roles doesn't have to mean chaos. Instead, it can reflect a rich, purposeful life when aligned

with calling and passion. You might use anecdotes about lessons learned in balancing your jobs (your career, parenting, elder care, church work, volunteering, etc.), offering tools for prioritizing and thriving in multifaceted roles.

2. Be Content with Book Sales.

- Celebrate the impact of each book sold and the stories of readers touched by your work.
- Shift focus from sales numbers to the deeper meaning of your message, trusting God with the results.
- Use creative and joyful ways to promote your books, such as storytelling, videos, or connecting with readers personally.
- Set realistic goals and recognize every milestone, however small, as progress.
- Explore and write about how contentment in creativity stems from purpose rather than profit. Include stories of small, unexpected moments of encouragement—a single reader's feedback that reaffirmed your calling—and reminded you to find joy in the process rather than just the outcome.

3. Be Content with a Busy Schedule.

- Start each day with gratitude and prayer, focusing on what is gained rather than lost in the busyness.
- Schedule intentional downtime and honor it as sacred.
- Practice presence by giving full attention to one task or person at a time.
- Simplify and prioritize by regularly asking, "What truly matters today?"
- Write about how busyness doesn't have to rob us of peace when we focus on purpose and prioritize what aligns with our values. Your stories might reflect how moments of stillness amid busyness became sources of strength and joy.

4. Embrace Peace Amid the Busyness.

- Pause throughout the day for short moments of silence and reflection.
- Incorporate breathing exercises or mindfulness to reset during hectic times.
- Keep visible reminders of peace (Scriptures, quotes, or photos) in your workspaces.
- Build a support system of family and friends who encourage rest and renewal.
- Write about learning to "breathe peace" into the chaos, including tips for finding rest in the midst of a full life. Journal about personal rituals or habits that bring calm, weaving these into a broader message of trusting God's rhythm over the world's rush.

5. Don't Worry About Money for Retirement or the Future.

- Trust God's provision by meditating on promises like those in Matthew 6:33–34.
- Take small, proactive steps in financial planning while releasing anxiety over outcomes.
- Find joy in giving and gratitude for what He has already given, practicing a mindset of abundance over scarcity.
- Reflect on how God has provided in unexpected ways in the past.
- Share how surrendering financial worries can transform your perspective, reminding yourself that God's provision often comes in surprising and creative ways. Stories of trust and provision may inspire you to release fear and embrace faith.

6. Sleep Well.

- Create an evening routine that promotes relaxation (journaling, reading Scripture, or listening to calming music).

- Avoid over-scheduling the evening hours, allowing time to unwind.
- Use prayer as a way to "hand over" the day's burdens to God before sleep.
- Incorporate gratitude reflection at bedtime, listing blessings from the day.
- Reflect on how rest is an act of trust, reminding yourself that even Jesus rested. Practical tips for cultivating a peaceful mind before sleep could resonate when you're struggling to rest amid a busy life.

7. Laugh Often.

- Spend time with people who bring joy and laughter.
- Find humor in everyday moments, even the challenging ones.
- Regularly watch or read something lighthearted.
- Remind yourself that laughter is part of God's gift of abundant life.
- Write about the healing power of laughter, sharing humorous and heartwarming stories from your life. Remind yourself that laughter is not just an escape but a way to engage with life's beauty and joy, even in hard times

SECTION TWO
LIVING WITH LIMITS

5

WHEN LIFE DOESN'T GO AS PLANNED

"Contentment derives from long and painful seasons of pain, sorrow and discomfort." **—David Kaywood**[7]

You had it mapped out.

The timeline. The goals. The dreams, carefully lined in a row—everything aligned perfectly, step after step after step.

But then ...

The phone rang. The diagnosis came. The job fell through. The relationship shifted. The house burned down. The accusations began. The hurricane hit. The drunk driver drove directly into the car. The story changed.

You were left staring at the pieces of a plan that didn't happen. Left hearing silence where music previously played.

I didn't plan for brain damage. Or seizures. Or the silent frustrations that follow. I didn't plan for constant reminders of weakness.

---

7 David Kaywood, *A Call to Contentment: Pursuing Godly Satisfaction in a Restless World* (Fearn, Scotland: Christian Focus Publications Ltd., 2024), 49.

But here I am. And here you are.

Somehow contentment can still meet us here when life doesn't go as planned. Not because I got what I wanted. Not because I pretended it was fine. But because I opened my hands and asked a better question:

"How do I live well, even here?"

I didn't have to love the plan to find contentment in the present. I glanced through a situation and concluded, "God is with me, even here."

And then—faintly, softly—a new harmony rose from the quiet.

Different than I expected. Still beautiful.

Contentment doesn't always restore the old song.

Sometimes it teaches us to sing a new one.

Letting Go of the Ideal

There's a temptation to wait for life to fix itself before we breathe again. To exist with the maybe-one-day mentality. To hold our breath until the plan returns to schedule.

But life doesn't need to be endured that way.

And contentment isn't found in someday.

It's found in today. In the mess, in the grief, in the rearranged calendar and rewritten dreams. During the waiting. Amid the anger. Through the tears. Among the wounds.

A New Kind of Trust

When life doesn't go as planned, we're invited to trust again, differently.

Not a surface-level, easy trust. But a deep, quiet one. The kind that whispers, "Even now, I believe there's something sacred here."

Contentment isn't denying pain. It's refusing to let pain become your only story.

We don't have to love the detour. But we can still live it well. We don't have to feel okay. But we can still choose peace. We don't have to understand the why. But we can still cling to the Who.

The plan changed. But the presence of God didn't.

And really, isn't that more than enough?

When Contentment Feels Out of Reach

There are days—maybe even whole seasons—when contentment seems like a distant star in the night sky. You can see its light, but you can't touch it. You hear stories about peace and gratitude and thankfulness, but your mind is crowded with disappointment, anxiety, or unmet longings. You wonder: Is something wrong with me? Am I missing the secret everyone else has figured out?

Contentment doesn't always come easily. Sometimes it feels more like a discipline than a gift, more like a battle than a blessing. It's okay to admit that. Contentment doesn't mean denying pain or pretending everything is fine. It means anchoring ourselves in a deeper truth even when our emotions are swirling. When life hurts, when prayers seem unanswered, when dreams are deferred, we can still whisper a fragile yes to the presence of God in the middle of it all.

You are not alone if contentment feels elusive. It's not a sign of failure—it's a sign that you're human. The path to contentment is uneven. There are days when you will feel it and days when you won't. But the invitation remains. Even in sorrow. Even in silence. Even when you're still waiting for healing, resolution, or clarity. Contentment, in those moments, is not found in a feeling—it's found in trust.

When Life is Hard, Pain Comes, and Hope Seems Distant

Contentment doesn't ignore pain; it endures it. The Father says, "Even though you walk through the valley, I am with you" (Psalm 23:4). Jesus reminds us, "In this world, you will have trouble. But take heart! I have overcome the world" (John 16:33). The Spirit groans with us when words fail, interceding on our behalf (Romans 8:26). When life feels unbearable, contentment isn't pretending everything is fine; it's trusting that God is still good.

Pain refines us, reminding us that contentment isn't circumstantial. It's learning to say with Paul, "I have learned the secret of being content ... I can do all this through Him who gives me strength" (Philippians 4:12–13). Contentment leans into God's strength when our own is gone, finding peace in His promises and hope in His eternal perspective.

The Week That Changed Everything: A Story of True Contentment

We walk toward Easter every year. The calendar leads us there, but so does our heart—the longing, the wondering, the remembering.

I've walked through this week more times than I can count. Palm Sunday. Maundy Thursday. Good Friday. Silent Saturday. Resurrection Sunday. I've heard and preached the sermons, written the reflections, spoken the words in communion lines and altar calls. Still, I find myself asking, "What can I still learn? How can I be changed again?"

This year I saw the week through the lens of contentment—not the shallow version we often settle for but the real, soul-deep kind. The kind that Jesus lived.

Jesus wasn't chasing more. He wasn't striving to impress. He wasn't afraid of discomfort, betrayal, or pain. He wasn't running from reality. He walked into it—fully surrendered, fully present, and deeply content in His Father's will.

Here's what that week teaches me about contentment:

Palm Sunday: Contentment in Identity

- Jesus entered the city not on a war horse, but on a donkey. Not with pride, but with prophecy.
- He didn't need the approval of the crowd waving palm branches. He knew who He was, and that was enough.
- When I know who I am in Christ, I don't need to prove anything. I can rest in His truth, not chase public applause.

Monday: Contentment in Righteous Disruption

- Jesus overturned tables in the temple. He wasn't trying to keep the peace. He wanted real peace to return and take the place of a religious enterprise crowded in its place. He was doing the right thing, even when it made people uncomfortable.
- Contentment isn't passive—it has courage. It speaks up. It acts without fear because it trusts the Father's heart.

Tuesday: Contentment in Teaching the Truth

- They tried to trap Him with questions. They tried to twist His words. But He didn't panic. He taught with clarity, even when He was misunderstood.
- I don't have to control how others respond. I can speak truth with peace, rooted in something deeper than popularity.

Wednesday: Contentment in the Shadows

- The Gospels are quiet on this day. But we know Judas was plotting.
- Jesus didn't rush. He wasn't anxious. He was still.
- Some days are filled with silence and shadows. But even then, God is at work. I can rest in the quiet.

Thursday: Contentment in Serving and Surrendering

- He washed feet. He broke bread. He prayed in agony.
- And then He said, "Not my will, but Yours."
- Real contentment doesn't mean the pain goes away—it means I trust God more than I trust my desire for comfort.

Friday: Contentment in the Cross

- The world saw failure. Defeat. But Jesus saw fulfillment.

- "It is finished," He said, not as a cry of despair but of victory.
- Contentment looks like faith in the middle of the storm. It looks like hope nailed to a cross, still believing.

Saturday: Contentment in the Waiting

- No miracles. No movement. Just silence.
- But even then, God was not absent.
- I can wait, even in the dark, knowing that resurrection is coming.

Sunday: Contentment in New Life

- He didn't come back with fanfare. He came back with peace.
- He walked with His friends. Ate with them. Spoke their names.
- Contentment doesn't shout. It simply lives in resurrection joy, steady and sure.

As we walk through the Holy Week story once again, maybe we're searching for what has been there all along—not in escape or comfort, not in popularity or wealth, not with applause and approval, but in Jesus' quiet surrender. In His holy trust. In His willingness to live each moment with purpose, presence, and peace.

This is where contentment lives—not in avoiding pain but in walking through it with Jesus.

A Letter to Me Concerning a Medication No Longer Covered By Insurance

Dear Self:

Take a deep breath.

You've been here before. Not in this exact spot, no. But you've faced storms. You've walked unfamiliar roads. And you've found a way to stay kind, to remain steady, to keep the light on even when the power threatened to go out.

This situation—your insurance company refusing to cover the medication that has worked for you for decades—is frustrating. It's more than frustrating, actually. It feels personal. It feels unfair. It feels like a system designed to save dollars is willing to risk your well-being in the process.

You want to be angry. You want to shout. You want to cry. And it's okay to feel all of that. But, dear self, don't become bitter. Don't lose your peace. Don't let this moment shape you into someone you are not. You are calm. You are kind. You are trusting—even when it's hard.

Still, ask the questions.

Ask why a company or a government would push someone away from what works. From what's safe. From what allows them to live a stable, meaningful life. Ask why the people making decisions aren't required to understand the ripple effect those decisions create—not only in the life of the patient but also in the lives of their caregivers, their families, their communities.

Have big business and big government become so entangled in their own agendas that they've forgotten the human lives affected by every policy and every profit margin?

Ask who is thinking about us—the patients who live with conditions like epilepsy. The caregivers who wake up at night to check on us. The doctors who spent years finding the right treatment plan, only to see it overridden by bureaucracy.

Is it all about money? Is anyone in the boardrooms or the legislative halls really listening to stories like mine?

You're not alone, dear self. There are so many others quietly navigating situations like yours—people living through worse, people who are tired, who are praying, who are trying to stay kind in a world that often rewards the opposite.

Keep asking the hard questions. Keep raising your voice—but do it with grace. Keep standing firm—but stay soft. Keep trusting that God sees this, knows this, and is with you in it.

And most of all, stay you. The you who chooses hope over hate. Peace over panic. Kindness over cruelty.

Because the world needs more of that.

With peace,

Me

6 THE GIFT OF LIMITS

"No matter how determined or hardworking we are, we depend entirely on the Lord to establish the work of our hands. Even the seemingly passive activity of a good night's sleep is a gift from the Lord!" **—Megan Hill**[8]

My neurologist read my story about the view from the roof. He reminded me—again—I wasn't allowed up there. Even if I loved the sight, I didn't belong there. Not to clean gutters. Not to grab fallen limbs. Not anymore.

I told him about riding a roller coaster, how it felt different this time—unsettling, unlike all my other rides through the years. He reminded me—not as gently as I'm phrasing it here—I should never ride anything like that again.

I live a life of limits. Medication and sleep schedules. Sunglasses on bright days. Avoiding flashing lights at concerts and stadiums. Staying cautious in heat, in stress, in long nights that stretch too far.

Daily reminders whisper: *You can't. You shouldn't. Not anymore.*

For a long time, I heard those whispers as losses—as restrictions, as lesser-than.

---

8 Megan Hill, *Contentment: Seeing God's Goodness: 31-Day Devotionals for Life*, (Phillipsburg, NJ: P&R Publishing, 2018), 35.

But slowly, painfully, kindly—I've begun to see them differently. Limits are not always punishments. Sometimes they're invitations: To slow down. To listen more closely. To be fully present in the small spaces I used to rush past.

Maybe the life I wanted isn't the only good life. Maybe this limited one holds a quiet, sacred kind of abundance—one I would've missed if I kept rushing past it.

Limits aren't the enemy. They're often the invitation.

We tend to resist the word *limit*. We push against boundaries. We strive to break barriers. We equate more with better and faster with success.

But what if our limits aren't curses?

What if they're gifts?

I've felt the sting of limitation. My body reminds me every day with its possibility of seizures, the reality of brain damage, the weariness that lingers uninvited but persistent.

My mind can't go as fast as it once did. My schedule shouldn't stay as full. My achievements won't match the world's expectations.

But maybe that's okay.

Debbie and I were walking through our neighborhood when movement caught my eye. At first, I thought I saw one rabbit—the usual. But this was different. Eight rabbits! Eight rabbits at full speed at the same time. Moving together in the same direction, same velocity, same mission. They hopped through one front yard, disappeared into a nearby backyard, and then reappeared together again.

I'd never seen that before. So many. All at once. All together.

I couldn't help but think—shouldn't people move through life like that? Through the yards of uncertainty and the neighborhoods of fear, not alone but together? In step with our tribe?

Contentment has a way of finding us when we're not hopping alone.

When Less Becomes More

Our limits slow us down.

And in the slowing, we begin to see.

We begin to notice things we used to rush past. We hear voices we once ignored—including our own. We let go of proving, and begin the quiet work of becoming.

Limitations strip us—yes.

But they also ground us. They draw us back to our need for grace.

God Meets You Where You Are

God isn't asking for endless output. He isn't waiting for you to measure up. He meets you in your limits—not beyond them.

Jesus, who took on flesh, embraced limits.

He got tired.

He withdrew.

He didn't heal everyone.

He didn't preach to every crowd.

And He was content—in perfect communion with His Father.

Embracing the Gift

We don't have to glorify pain. But we can honor the sacred invitation in it.

Limits teach us to rest. To depend. To release.

They invite us into rhythms of grace rather than pressure. They remind us: You are not God. You don't have to be.

When I stopped fighting every limitation, I began to live more freely. Not less purposefully—but more. Because freedom isn't found in having no limits. It's found in trusting the One who works within them.

Your limits aren't the extent of your usefulness. They might just be the beginning of your transformation.

Living in the Rhythm of Contentment

Contentment isn't a passive feeling—it's a deliberate practice, a rhythm we choose to live by. Life often leaves us longing for more: a better future, a different past, a more fulfilling present. But in those moments, we must pause. Not to rush past our restlessness or silence our pain, but to listen.

In my journey, there have been seasons when contentment felt far away. Have you ever wanted to rewind time, to regain what you thought you had lost? But over the years, we can learn that contentment isn't about avoiding grief or ignoring dreams; it's about learning to live fully in what is.

Even with limitations. Even with wounds. Even with questions.

But how? What are some ways to learn that, to craft limitations which help us live fully in what is?

1. **Practice Presence:** The practice of contentment begins with presence. We must pause long enough to truly see where we are. As I reflect on the Psalms, I find comfort in David's honesty—he wasn't content because his life was perfect; he was content because he chose to trust God in the imperfection.

2. **Embrace Gratitude:** Gratitude shifts the soul's perspective. It's not a denial of life's challenges but an acknowledgment of the blessings we often overlook. When I practice gratitude, I'm reminded that the moments I have are enough. My scars? They are reminders of grace.

3. **Find Contentment in Relationships:** Contentment thrives in community. Sharing stories, bearing burdens, and walking together—this is where joy lives. As I wrote in *Things We've Handed Down*, we leave legacies not through wealth or accomplishments but through love, wisdom, and faith.

4. **Trust in God's Sufficiency:** When I feel the pull of discontentment, I remind myself of Paul's words: "I have learned the secret of being content in any and every situation, whether well fed or hungry, whether living in plenty or in want. I can do all this through Him who gives me strength" (Philippians 4:12–13). Contentment isn't about self-sufficiency but about resting in the sufficiency of Christ.

5. **Live the Practice Daily:** Contentment isn't a one-time choice; it's a daily rhythm. Like breathing deeply, it requires intentionality. Start small: write a list of blessings, pause in the chaos, choose kindness over comparison.

In the pursuit of contentment, we're reminded that we were never meant to chase after "enough" on our own. True contentment whispers to us in the stillness: "You already have enough, because God is enough."

So, let us practice this rhythm together. Let us pause. Reflect. Find balance in the moments we've been given. And as we live this way, we will discover that contentment isn't just something we long for—it's a gift we can live in every day.

Contentment: A Life Framed by Twenty "C" Words

True contentment is not about acquiring more but about living fully in God's presence, purpose, and peace. It's a journey shaped by how we think, act, and respond to life's opportunities and challenges. The following twenty "C" words offer practical and encouraging steps to cultivate a contented life that glorifies God and enriches those around us. Process each word and consider which limitations can supply you with opportunities for your future life.

1. **Cadence:** Life has a God-designed rhythm. Contentment grows when we honor this balance—working diligently, resting intentionally, and worshiping faithfully. When we align with the cadence of creation, we find peace in trusting God's perfect timing for all things.

2. **Calmness:** A calm heart is a haven of peace. Calmness comes when we pause amid chaos, choosing stillness over panic. It's a choice to anchor ourselves in God's promises and trust His plan, no matter the circumstances swirling around us.

3. **Care:** Care is both a calling and a gift. Contentment deepens as we invest in loving others, stewarding creation, and tending to our own well-being. When we reflect God's compassion through acts of kindness, we experience the joy of His presence.

4. **Casually:** Living casually doesn't mean neglecting responsibilities but releasing the constant need to strive for perfection. By slowing down and appreciating the small moments, we embrace a spirit of gratitude and learn to savor the blessings of today.

5. **Caution:** Caution is a guardrail for wise living. Contentment doesn't mean rushing ahead recklessly but seeking God's wisdom in every decision. By pausing to reflect, pray, and discern, we protect ourselves from unnecessary regret and align our steps with His will.

6. **Celebration:** Celebration reminds us to rejoice in what God has done. Contentment flourishes when we celebrate life's milestones, relationships, and simple joys. Gratitude grows as we remember His faithfulness and give thanks for His abundant blessings.

7. **Centering:** Centering ourselves in God's truth keeps us grounded. Through prayer, Scripture, and reflection, we realign our hearts with His purposes. When we are centered, we focus on eternal priorities rather than fleeting distractions.

8. **Character:** Contentment flows from who we are becoming in Christ. Building strong character means choosing integrity, humility, and love, even when no one else is watching. True peace is found in living authentically and reflecting God's image.

9. **Cheerfulness:** A cheerful heart overflows with gratitude and joy. Cheerfulness isn't about denying struggles but choosing to focus on life's beauty and blessings. A cheerful attitude lifts our spirits and spreads encouragement to those around us.

10. **Comfort:** God's comfort is our refuge in times of need. Contentment grows as we rest in His presence, knowing He understands our struggles and carries our burdens. His comfort assures us that we are never alone, even in life's hardest moments.

11. **Community:** We were created for connection. Contentment is enriched through meaningful relationships and shared experiences. Leaning on community provides support, accountability, and joy as we journey together, reminding us that we are stronger when united.

12. **Competence:** Contentment blossoms when we use our gifts and grow in our skills. Developing competence isn't about seeking approval, but stewarding what God has entrusted to us. Confidence grows as we faithfully serve others with excellence and humility.

13. **Composure:** Composure is the ability to remain steady in life's storms. It's a sign of trust in God's sovereignty, allowing us to respond thoughtfully instead of reacting impulsively. Contentment grows as we let God's peace guard our hearts and minds.

14. **Confidence:** Confidence is rooted in knowing our identity in Christ. It's the assurance that God is for us and working all things for good. Living confidently allows us to walk boldly into each day, trusting His promises and provision.

15. **Consistency:** Contentment requires faithfulness in the small things. Consistency in our routines—prayer, work, relationships—builds trust and momentum. By showing up daily with a spirit of faithfulness, we cultivate habits that honor God and enrich our lives.

16. **Conviction:** Living with conviction means staying true to our beliefs, even when it's inconvenient or unpopular. Conviction gives us purpose and clarity, reminding us of who we are and why we do what we do. Contentment grows when our actions align with God's truth.

17. **Cooperation:** Cooperation teaches us the beauty of teamwork. Contentment is found when we work together, share responsibilities, and celebrate others' strengths. By embracing humility and unity, we build stronger relationships and accomplish more than we could alone.

18. **Courage:** Courage is essential for contentment, as life often requires us to step into the unknown. Trusting God over our fears allows us to move forward with hope and determination, knowing He will never leave us nor forsake us.

19. **Creativity:** Creativity helps us see God's fingerprints everywhere. Whether through art, innovation, or problem-solving, expressing creativity reflects His image in us. By creating, we experience the joy of discovery and bring beauty into the world.

20. **Curiosity:** Curiosity keeps us engaged and grateful. Instead of dwelling on what we lack, we explore life with wonder, asking, "What can I learn here?" Staying curious opens our minds to new opportunities and perspectives, expanding our capacity for gratitude and growth.

By arranging limitations to harness these twenty "C" words, we create a life of deep contentment—a life centered on God, enriched by relationships, and marked by peace and purpose.

7

PRACTICING PRESENCE

"It is a matter of dedicating to God the world within our reach."
—Andrew Peterson[9]

Those words from Chapter Six are like a collection of brands. The aisle is covered with numerous labels. Every product, each word, emphasized the value of this merchandise. Contentment—with comfort, with competence, with consistency—is obtainable now. Here. For us.

But where? How far away?

Contentment lives where your feet are.

We just might need to stop in the lane of life long enough to grab it.

Why is that so hard? We know we should. We think about it. We try for a while. But we suddenly become obsessed with what is missing, what we aren't, who we wish we were, what we wish we had. And we fail to notice our obsessions.

We are people in a hurry. Scrolling. Clicking. Moving.

Multitasking our way through days we barely remember. But the truth is—multitasking is a myth. We're not doing many things at once; we're doing one thing poorly at a time.

9 Andrew Peterson, *Adorning the Dark: Thoughts on Community, Calling, and the Mystery of Making* (Brentwood, TN: B & H Publishing, 2019), 18.

We talk about living in the moment, but often, we're just surviving it—barely aware, barely grounded, barely here.

Contentment isn't found in the next thing. It's found in the now thing.

The moment you're in.

The breath you just took.

The prayer you just prayed.

The weakness you still have.

The possibilities you still hope for.

The person right beside you.

The grace that's holding you—still.

What We Miss While We Rush

When we're always moving, we miss the sacredness of the ordinary. The way the sunlight beams through a window. The quiet encouragement of a friend. The sound of laughter in another room.

We miss the God who meets us in small things. Because we're waiting for something big.

But presence isn't passive.

It's a spiritual practice. It takes intention to slow down, to stay, to see.

Choosing to Be Here

I've learned this the hard way.

When I stare at the schedule and look too far ahead. When I plan and plan and plan, while forgetting what is in that place at that time for a reason.

When the possibility of a seizure forces me to sit still. When brain fog makes words hard to find. When I can't keep up with the demands I once prided myself on.

When days of pastoring became decades. When children had children of their own. When a book I wrote became an old book. When a picture I glanced at again reminded me of what felt like a previous existence.

When I find it difficult to do what I previously found simple. When I watch others find it simple to do what I cannot do.

I must choose: Resent the stillness, or receive it. Stop the hurry. Steer off the fast lane. Take the turn. Hit the brakes. Pull over. Turn off the engine.

I chose—often imperfectly—to receive it.

And in that stillness, I meet presence.

God's presence.

My own presence.

The presence of others, unfiltered and real.

The Deep Work of Noticing

Contentment grows in the soil of attention.

It thrives when we look, when we listen, when we breathe.

To practice presence is to say, "This moment matters. I will be in it."

Not the next big thing. Not the regret behind you. This. This breath. This grace. This encounter with the eternal now. This person, this prayer, this song, this place.

Only today. Not tomorrow.

Now. Not then.

Instead of chasing contentment, we have to slow down enough to let it find us.

As I'm writing this I decided to practice what I suggest. So, I stopped staring at a screen and typing sentences. I glanced over the table, that place I eat food, that place we meet together as a family and talk, listen, share, care.

It was just a glance.

It wasn't a big moment.

But I remembered another moment—a big moment that didn't seem so large at the time.

I recalled sitting at the dinner table with my family. The conversation wasn't profound, the food wasn't fancy. But I remembered looking around, swallowing more than food. I felt something stir deep within me—a quiet joy, a sense that this, right here, was enough.

For years, I had chased contentment in accomplishments, possessions, and plans. But there it was, in that time and place, the simplicity of being with the people I love, breaking bread together, laughing at a joke that didn't even make sense, making eye contact announced genuine care, realizing that moment would never be repeated.

Contentment didn't need more. It just needed me to notice.

I'm glad I did.

I pray I notice more.

It takes practice. Practicing the presence—our own, our friends and family, our God's—each presence there. Each of us becoming more aware. Each day, event, place, story—practicing a recognition of reality.

Isn't that a wonderful opportunity for us to find contentment? Letting a theological belief about the Holy Spirit finding a dwelling place within us and around us—isn't that too intriguing for us to ignore?

Think about it: God with us, God within us, calm and content. All we need is here. Not a faraway god, but a right here, right now, listening, loving, caring, guiding, providing, forgiving, empowering, healing, smiling, assuring, holding, nodding, confronting, promising, teaching, mentoring God.

One of our grandchildren recently felt afraid. Tears began to wet her face. She began calling for her parents who were away. I didn't know the cause; I only saw the effect. So I didn't have an answer. But I had this: myself. To be there. To stay there. And to hold a grandchild's little body with my old arms which felt large.

That's what God wants to do.

His presence creates a sense of contentment to replace our fear. Let us let Him.

Finding Contentment in the Midst of Exhaustion

Finding contentment in the midst of exhaustion—whether emotional, mental, or physical—requires a shift in perspective. It's not about escaping the exhaustion but learning to embrace grace within it. Here are a few simple, deep, practical reflections to guide you:

1. **Pause and Acknowledge:** Stop running for a moment. Breathe. Acknowledge where you are. Sometimes contentment begins by admitting your weariness instead of pretending it doesn't exist. Say it out loud if you need to: "I'm tired, and that's okay." This honesty invites God's presence into your weakness.

   "Come to me, all you who are weary and burdened, and I will give you rest." (Matthew 11:28)

2. **Reframe Your Perspective:** Contentment isn't found in ideal circumstances; it's found in trusting God amidst imperfect ones. Look at your current state not as defeat but as an opportunity to depend on His strength. Shift from asking, "Why am I so drained?" to "How can I find grace here?"

3. **Simplify Your Focus:** When life feels overwhelming, choose one small thing to hold onto. Maybe it's a verse like Philippians 4:11–13, or a simple prayer: "God, help me rest in You." Let go of the clutter in your mind and focus on one truth—His grace is sufficient.

4. **Find a Sacred Rhythm:** Contentment grows when you find sustainable rhythms of rest and renewal. Create space for short, intentional moments of stillness each day. Sit quietly, go for a slow walk, or listen to a song that soothes your soul. Let these rhythms remind you that contentment is cultivated over time, not rushed.

5. **Stay Connected:** Isolation often amplifies exhaustion. Reach out to someone—a friend, a mentor, or a loved one—and share your heart. You don't need to have all the answers; just let their presence remind you that you're not alone.

6. **Look for the Little Joys:** Even in exhaustion, there are glimpses of beauty. A sunrise. A kind word. A moment of stillness. Train your eyes to see these small gifts, and let them become reminders of God's faithfulness.

   "The Lord is my shepherd; I lack nothing." (Psalm 23:1)

7. **Rest in God's Sovereignty:** Finally, let go of what you can't control. Trust that God is holding you, even when you feel too weak to hold onto Him. Rest in this truth: His love for you isn't based on your strength but on His.

Exhaustion doesn't define you. Grace does. Let contentment arise not from what you accomplish but from the One who holds you in your weariness. One step, one prayer, one breath at a time.

8 WHEN YOU FEEL LEFT BEHIND

> *"It can be tempting to become discontent when it feels like our work goes unnoticed."* **—Megan Hill**[10]

Unwanted. Unloved. Unseen. Unappreciated. Unacknowledged. Unvalued. Undesired.

The words glared back from the screen, dark letters on a white background. No music. No noise. Just silence—and the sting of recognition.

The dry erase marker I'd used earlier still rested on the ledge below the board. I could hear it rolling slightly when someone shifted in their seat. Outside, a faint wind began to stir, brushing against the windows as if it wanted to come in. A chair creaked. Someone sniffed.

We sat still, staring and waiting. The students didn't know what we were waiting for. But they could feel those words were there for a reason. For several reasons.

Finally, I asked, "Which words describe how you felt as a child? Why? Which words describe how you feel now? Why? How has your life been shaped by un-words like these?"

---

10 Megan Hill, *Contentment: Seeing God's Goodness* (Phillipsburg, NJ: P&R Publishing, 2018), 77.

I invited them to begin journaling. Screens lit up around the room. Fingers tapped softly on keyboards and phone screens—a quiet rhythm filling the air. The silence thickened.

After a time, I said, "If you want to talk about those words, I invite you to speak now."

The silence broke—slowly, painfully.

And then it poured out.

Tears first, then words. Anger, hurt, compassion, confession. Stories of rejection, of abuse, of always seeking approval but never receiving it. Stories of being left out, last picked, not smart enough, not spiritual enough, not slim enough, not athletic enough. Of being every boy's best friend but no boy's girlfriend. Of watching others understand lessons instantly while they sat lost and ashamed. Of trying to disappear by skipping meals. Of living in the shadow of a perfect sibling.

One student stood. His face flushed red, fists clenched tight. He marched to the board, grabbed the marker, and slashed a line over each word. Then another line. Then another. The squeak of the marker against the board was sharp, almost angry. He threw it to the ground, the clatter echoing in the silence.

Another student whispered, "I gave myself the name 'Invisible.' Because no one ever notices me, and no one seems to care." Her voice didn't shake. It was calm—too calm. Everyone leaned in to hear her, as if her quiet confession carried more weight than shouting ever could. The name had long since become her identity.

A girl in the back spoke for the first time all semester. Just four words: "I feel left behind."

Another boy's voice cracked as he spoke of death—again and again and again. Not in past tense. Present tense. Losses still fresh. Still bleeding. He believed more losses would follow.

The stories kept coming—even after class officially ended. No one moved toward the door. Not yet.

And we didn't let them leave with just pain.

We began the work—naming the truth, walking toward healing, rewriting their stories. Slowly. Tenderly.

What about you? If you were in that class, which *un-words* would describe you? Which would remind you of your past? Which ones still affect your present? What would you write in your journal? What would you say if you felt safe enough to speak?

Some wounds are loud. Others are silent. But nearly all of them whisper the same thing. *You've been left behind.* By friends. By family. By success. By hope. And maybe, you think, by God.

You look around and it feels like everyone else is moving forward. They're getting promotions. They're launching books. Their churches are growing. Their families are celebrating milestones.

And you are ... still waiting.

Still hoping. Still trying. Still wondering why your story isn't moving forward like theirs.

Comparison quietly convinces us we're behind. As if life is a race. As if there's one right pace. As if fulfillment only comes once we catch up.

But contentment doesn't live in someone else's timeline.

It lives in your own sacred becoming.

The Noise of "Not Enough"

It doesn't take long to feel the noise: the social scroll, the ministry metrics, the endless highlight reels.

It's loud. It's constant. It's convincing.

And if we're not careful, it tells us a lie: "You've missed it. You should be more by now."

But more doesn't equal better. And behind doesn't mean broken.

The Beautiful Work of Becoming

I've felt left behind. Haven't you?

In the near. In the far away. In the doing. In the going. In the waiting.

It's easy to believe the lie that others are where I'm supposed to be.

But slowly, I've learned this truth: Contentment doesn't come from catching up. It comes from waking up—to where I am, to what God is doing here.

Growth isn't always visible.

Sometimes it's slow.

Sometimes it's invisible.

But that doesn't make it less real.

A Different Kind of Timeline

God doesn't run on urgency. He works through presence. He shapes souls in silence, in obscurity, in patience.

You're not missing your moment.

You're living in it.

Even if it's quiet.

Even if it feels slow.

Even if you're still waiting for what others seem to already have.

You are not behind. You're becoming. And that's a story worth living.

The Gift in the Unseen

Contentment often feels elusive, like a gift just out of reach. We chase it through promotions, possessions, and plans, only to find it slipping away. But what if contentment isn't something we chase? What if it's something we uncover—hidden in the moments we too often overlook?

I remember a season of waiting, one marked by uncertainty and questions. My mind, altered by brain injury, couldn't process life the way it once did. I was tempted to define my worth by what I lost. But in those quiet, ordinary moments, God began to whisper something new: "Chris, look again."

It was in the waiting—when life felt incomplete—that I discovered contentment was never about perfection or completion. It was about presence.

And sometimes our presence isn't where we frequently find ourselves.

I don't go to the grocery store often, but when I do I'm reminded how much happens there beyond shopping.

One day, as I neared the checkout for my quick trip, I had just a couple of items. The man in front of me had many. He glanced at my basket and insisted I go ahead of him. "Sir," he said, "you shouldn't have to wait for all this. Step in front of me."

I resisted at first. He wouldn't hear it. And just like that, kindness opened a conversation. We didn't know each other before that day, and I doubt we'll meet again. But for a few minutes, we were friends.

Then we both noticed something—the woman ahead of us had left without some of her groceries. We called her, and she came back to retrieve them.

Sometimes that's what community does: notices what's missing, calls out in care, and makes sure others leave whole.

Contentment often comes in those unexpected checkout lines of life—when kindness rearranges the order and connection makes the wait worthwhile.

The Lesson of the Empty Seat

The chair in the corner of the room was empty.

I remembered how often I would rush past it in the old days, never stopping long enough to sit, breathe, or simply be. That chair became a symbol for me in the months after my life slowed down.

One day, I finally sat down.

It wasn't comfortable at first—this idea of stillness. My mind wanted to wander, my body wanted to move. But I stayed. And as I did, I began to hear the gentle voice of contentment: "You don't have to go anywhere to find joy. You don't need to fix everything to find peace. Just sit. Just be. I am here."

The Student Who Taught Me

He came to my office, his face weary from carrying burdens too heavy for his young shoulders. He spoke of dreams that hadn't worked out, relationships that had left him broken, a life that seemed stuck in the in-between.

I listened, offering what little advice I could. But then he said something that stayed with me: "Even though it hurts, I'm trying to be grateful. I think that's where God is teaching me to rest."

His words echoed in my heart long after he left. Gratitude in the pain. Rest in the unknown. Contentment not in having all the answers, but in trusting the One who does.

9
THE HIDDEN PLACES

"Can you remember a time in your life when you felt blissfully contented, even for just a few moments? What put an end to it?"
— **Anne Woodcock**[11]

Roots grow deep in silence.

There are seasons when it feels like the world has moved on without you. No headlines. No applause. No visible fruit. Just the quiet, hidden work of staying faithful.

It's easy to believe what's unseen is unimportant. That if no one's noticing, it must not matter. But the opposite is true in the Kingdom of God.

Sacred Spaces with No Spotlight

Jesus spent thirty years in obscurity before three years in ministry. David served in the shadows long before he ever held a crown. Paul spent time in the wilderness before becoming a missionary.

We forget this part of their stories. The long, hidden stretches. The chapters without miracles or microphones.

But those seasons weren't wasted.

They were formative.

11 Anne Woodcock, *Contentment: Healing the Hunger of Our Hearts* (Epsom, Surrey, England: The Good Book Company, 2008), 7.

Roots Before Fruit

A tree doesn't grow tall unless its roots go deep.

And roots grow in the dark.

Contentment in the hidden places is saying, "Even if no one sees this, even if it's slow, I will still show up."

You write the sermon. You serve the people. You take the medication. You hold the hand. You clean the kitchen. You read the book. You research the topic. You listen to a friend. You set up the chairs. You take down the chairs. You listen to another friend. You pray the prayer—again.

And heaven sees.

God sees.

Real Growth is Often Invisible

The world measures growth by visibility. But spiritual growth is often quiet. It shows up in patience. In surrender. In peace that doesn't make sense. In the refusal to quit.

I've lived through long seasons where nothing looked impressive. Low numbers. Few opportunities. Quiet progress. But in those hidden places, I've found something deeper: A contentment not dependent on recognition. A joy not built on outcome.

Becoming in the Background

You're still becoming, even when the world doesn't clap. You're still valuable, even when your work is small and unseen. You're still loved, even when no one says your name.

Contentment in the hidden places isn't resignation. It's revelation: I am not defined by how seen I am—but by how known I am by the One who loves me.

Jesus experienced that. He understood His why. He refused to let the whys of others get Him off course.

Slowly read the following Scripture passage which initiates Jesus' ministry at Nazareth, where He was ultimately rejected. Reflect on what happened, and how you can find value and contentment in your hidden places, your unknown places, your small places, your unseen places.

Jesus returned to Galilee in the power of the Spirit, and news about him spread through the whole countryside. He was teaching in their synagogues, and everyone praised him.

He went to Nazareth, where he had been brought up, and on the Sabbath day he went into the synagogue, as was his custom. He stood up to read, and the scroll of the prophet Isaiah was handed to him. Unrolling it, he found the place where it is written:

The Spirit of the LORD is on me,

because he has anointed me

to proclaim good news to the poor.

He has sent me to proclaim freedom for the prisoners

and recovery of sight for the blind,

to set the oppressed free,

to proclaim the year of the LORD's favor.

Then he rolled up the scroll, gave it back to the attendant and sat down. The eyes of everyone in the synagogue were fastened on him. He began by saying to them, *"Today this scripture is fulfilled in your hearing."* (Luke 4:14–21).

Jesus returned. He reminded the audience of His true purpose. They didn't get too excited. They eventually turned against Him. How did He respond? He stayed on course. When abused, when accused, when rejected, when ridiculed, when denied, when crucified: He remained who He was.

Content in the crowd. Content in the conflict. Content to the cross.

That true contentment feels like an elusive treasure. We chase it, name it, frame it in phrases like, "If only I had more" or "When life finally slows down."

But, as we've been considering, maybe contentment isn't something we pursue. Maybe it's something—or Someone—Who comes to us.

Jesus returned. Not just to Galilee. Not just to the synagogue. Not just to Isaiah's scroll.

He returned to show us what contentment looks like: not in striving, but in being Spirit-filled. Not in seeking fulfillment, but in seeing fulfillment standing before us in His place.

Jesus walked out of the wilderness empowered by the Holy Spirit. Not drained. Not restless. He didn't chase approval, success, or popularity. He knew who He was because He was filled with the One who gives identity.

And there's a lesson for us: contentment comes when we depend on the Spirit, not our achievements. We spend our days searching for power in promotions, possessions, and people's praise. But the Spirit invites us to stop. To breathe. To be. And to remember—we're already enough because He is enough.

"Today this scripture is fulfilled in your hearing." Jesus read these ancient words from Isaiah and proclaimed them alive. He wasn't waiting for another season, another solution, another moment.

And here's another lesson to learn from that story: contentment comes when we trust His promises. So often, we live in the "if onlys." If only the relationship healed. If only the finances balanced. If only the prayers were answered.

But Jesus didn't wait for responses to determine His contentment, His purpose, His security, His identity. He was who He was. He stayed who He was.

And He invites us to a deeper contentment. He invites us to believe the truth: the promises of God are fulfilled in Him. He is good news for the poor. Freedom for the captive. Sight for the blind. Even when life feels broken, He is whole. Even when we feel restless, He is rest.

Jesus didn't just proclaim the mission; He was the mission. He lived it. He fed the hungry, touched the untouchable, lifted the lowly.

Contentment wasn't about sitting still but about moving with purpose.

Contentment comes when we live beyond ourselves.

When we stop asking, "What can I get?" And start asking, "Who can I serve?"

In giving, we receive. In loving, we live. In serving, we find contentment that the world cannot offer.

Jesus returned to a place He knew, among people who had known Him. The dusty roads of Galilee were unchanged. The synagogue walls were the same. The scroll had not been rewritten.

But contentment doesn't wait for new roads, new walls, or new words. It doesn't stay on delay until Jesus comes to take us away. It's found when we recognize that Jesus has already returned to us.

He came to fulfill what we could not. To remind us who we are in Him. To call us into a mission greater than our own desires.

Contentment is Jesus coming into our Monday, our day to pay bills, our time stuck in traffic, our waiting, our craving, our rejection, our news of not getting the job, our sense of our true life's purpose being thrown in many different directions. Contentment is the face of Jesus right here in this place, right now in this situation.

Contentment isn't about circumstances.

It's about presence.

His presence.

So as we reflect on His return to Galilee, we find the invitation to return ourselves. Return to dependence on the Spirit. Return to trusting His promises. Return to serving His mission.

Because true contentment isn't found in the end of the world, but in the beginning of His kingdom. A kingdom that's already here. A kingdom which is also coming. A kingdom where Jesus lives and where Jesus returns. To us, for us, and now, through us.

Pause today. Let contentment settle in your soul. Not because everything is perfect, but because Jesus is present. Not because the road is easy, but because the Spirit empowers. Not because we're waiting for what's next, but because, in Him, everything we need is already fulfilled.

And, while no one may see it, the roots keep growing deep in the silence.

Practical Steps for Finding Hope in Contentment

1. **Pause and Reflect:** Begin by slowing down. Take a deep breath. Ask yourself: what gifts does today offer? Sometimes hope hides in the smallest of things—a kind word, a steady sunrise, a quiet prayer.
2. **Let Go of "What If":** So much of discontentment lives in the "what if" or the "if only." What if I hadn't made that mistake? If only I had more time, more money, more love. But healing begins when we release those weights and trust God with what is.
3. **Redefine Healing:** Healing isn't always about restoration to what once was. Sometimes it's about discovering new rhythms, new dreams, and new ways to live. Contentment grows when we stop measuring life by what we think we've lost and start living in the grace of what remains.
4. **Listen for God's Whisper:** Contentment is quieter than the noise of striving. It waits for us in prayer, in Scripture, in moments of stillness. It's in the promise of Psalm 46:10: "Be still, and know that I am God."
5. **Live Your Story with Gratitude:** Each of us is writing a story, one moment at a time. Contentment comes when we stop wishing for a different chapter and start giving thanks for the one we're in.

10

CONTENTMENT ISN'T COMFORTABLE

> *"We desire contentment, but only like a cure-all pill: take this pill, and in twenty minutes, you'll feel better. But contentment doesn't work instantly."* **—David Kaywood**[12]

Last week while writing a draft of this story, I sat in my neurologist's office.

The drive to Marietta always reminds me of my condition—the mountains fading in the rearview mirror, traffic tightening as I get closer to the city. I've made this trip for years, yet the mix of emotions never changes: gratitude for help, frustration at limitations, quiet prayers whispered under my breath.

The visit was routine but never easy. Questions about my anti-epileptic medications. Updates on how my brain damage can affect my eyesight. Notes about memory lapses—how they can sneak into conversations. Discussions of emotional stability, neuroplasticity, realistic hopes, and honest goals. Each detail confirmed what I already knew: healing is slow, and life is different now.

---

12 David Kaywood, *A Call to Contentment: Pursuing Godly Satisfaction in a Restless World* (Fearn, Scotland: Christian Focus Publications Ltd., 2024), 49.

Then, as always, came the prescription. New reminders of the reality of what is working with my dosage. And how I should be grateful.

None of it felt comfortable. But strangely, comfort isn't what I needed.

When I stepped into the elevator to leave, a man and his caregiver joined me. He was frail, eyes tired, holding on to the rail with one hand. We exchanged quiet greetings. He mentioned his condition. I asked questions. He answered. And in those few floors down to the main lobby, we shared something deeper than small talk—mutual recognition.

He smiled as we stepped out into the lobby. I asked if I could say a prayer for him. They both said yes—not only with their words, but with their facial expressions. They softly prayed aloud with me as I prayed. After the amen, we slowly went in different directions.

I don't remember his name. I don't know if I'll ever see him again. But I do know this: contentment met me there—in the discomfort, in the quiet elevator ride, in the simple gift of caring about someone else. It felt like another unexpected treat offered in a place I hadn't planned, nourishing in ways I didn't expect. A reminder that contentment isn't always comfortable, but it's always available.

What is your most comfortable chair—the one you sink into at the end of a long day? What couch holds your best naps, watching your favorite shows, your early morning prayers? What city brings comfort the moment you arrive—or even as you imagine being there? What event soothes your soul simply by happening or by being remembered?

Maybe it's a song that puts you at ease every time it plays. A photo that floods your mind with joy every time you see it. A name on your screen that makes you smile before you even answer the call.

Comfort lives in those moments. Familiar. Soft. Safe.

But contentment—the deep, steady kind this book invites you to discover—doesn't always live in those places. Sometimes it shows up when everything around you feels uncomfortable.

We expect contentment to look like comfort. To sound like calm waves slowly coming ashore. To feel like ease. But what if contentment is more than comfort? What if it's deeper than convenience?

We like comfort.

We chase convenience.

We naturally assume that ease equals success.

So when life gets hard, we assume we've missed something. We think contentment must have left the room. But maybe it hasn't. Maybe it's just showing up in a new form.

The Confusion Between Comfort and Peace

We confuse comfort with peace, but they're not the same.

Comfort is a feeling. Peace is a foundation.

Contentment doesn't mean we like everything about our current situation. It means we've chosen to trust God with it. It's not passive acceptance. It's active alignment.

What If It's Still Hard?

Sometimes we do all the "right" things. We pray, we read, we serve, we stay faithful. And life still feels hard.

That doesn't mean we've failed. It means we're human.

Even Jesus experienced sorrow. Even Paul pleaded with God to take the thorn away. Even the Psalms are filled with lament.

Contentment isn't pretending the pain isn't real. It's believing God is still good in the middle of it.

Stretching Toward Surrender

Debbie and I joined friends for a leadership retreat in the mountains. Or "hills" as some call them—but to me, they're mountains. And those mountains were my friends.

Every morning I was the first awake, walking outside to pray and breathe in the view. But I had a hope beyond the mountains and trees: I wanted to see a bear. More than anyone else in our group, I wanted to see a bear.

Others saw bears.

I didn't.

Even one night when our group went to dinner, a bear showed up before we arrived and left before we could see it. I searched. I asked others where they'd seen it. I followed their hints. No bear.

I saw clouds. I saw cows. I saw a nice place to walk and get ice cream. I saw beauty everywhere—but no bear.

It made me wonder: how often do we miss contentment because we're fixated on the one thing we didn't see? What if we chose to enjoy what's right in front of us instead?

The beauty around us doesn't need a bear to be enough.

Sometimes noticing beauty is hard. Sometimes, though, it isn't the hardest part. That difficult task might be living with, facing, enduring, accepting, and growing through the harder things that sit at the same table.

Growth is uncomfortable. Forgiveness is uncomfortable. Letting go is uncomfortable. Waiting is uncomfortable.

But contentment grows in that tension. Not in the resolution of it, but in the surrender to God within it.

We can learn to breathe here. Not because everything is easy, but because we're not alone in it.

Aligned with the Bigger Story

Contentment is alignment. With God's rhythm. With God's grace. With the reality that we aren't in control—and never had to be.

You may not feel comfortable right now, but you can still be deeply rooted. Still be at peace. Still live content. Because your worth isn't tied to how easy life is.

We often think contentment should feel soft, familiar, and easy. But Psalm 77 takes us into a different space—where contentment groans, cries out, and stretches its untiring hands toward a silent God.

This is the raw honesty of the faith journey: "I would not be comforted," Asaph says. And yet he prays. He remembers. He reflects. He doesn't deny the pain. He carries it to God. And in that process, something shifts.

The Psalmist's cry isn't neat. It's hoarse. His throat burns from sleepless nights. His fists clench, knuckles pale, as prayers tumble out—questions more than answers. In the silence, he feels the weight of being unheard ...until memory breaks through. His breath slows. His shoulders ease. He whispers stories of rescue: seas parting, lightning flashing, God leading unseen. The silence hasn't changed, but somehow it feels lighter now.

He chooses contentment—not because everything feels okay, but because he remembers the God who led His people through deep waters. The God whose footprints were unseen but whose faithfulness was unmistakable.

So, what if contentment doesn't begin with comfort? What if it begins with crying out, remembering, meditating, declaring?

Even when you can't feel it. Even when you're too tired to pretend. Even when comfort stays out of reach.

That's the sacred tension of contentment: it often arrives in the middle of the storm, not after it's over. It shows up when the footprints of God are invisible—but your faith walks forward anyway.

Pause now. Read Psalm 77 slowly. Let it read you. Let it guide you.

Psalm 77: A Psalm of Asaph

For the director of music. For Jeduthun.

I cried out to God for help;

I cried out to God to hear me.

When I was in distress, I sought the Lord;

at night I stretched out untiring hands,
and I would not be comforted.

I remembered you, God, and I groaned;
I meditated, and my spirit grew faint.
You kept my eyes from closing;
I was too troubled to speak.
I thought about the former days,
the years of long ago;
I remembered my songs in the night.
My heart meditated and my spirit asked:

"Will the LORD reject forever?
Will he never show his favor again?
Has his unfailing love vanished forever?
Has his promise failed for all time?
Has God forgotten to be merciful?
Has he in anger withheld his compassion?"

Then I thought, "To this I will appeal:
the years when the Most High stretched out his right hand.
I will remember the deeds of the LORD;
yes, I will remember your miracles of long ago.
I will consider all your works
and meditate on all your mighty deeds."

Your ways, God, are holy.
What god is as great as our God?
You are the God who performs miracles;

you display your power among the peoples.
With your mighty arm you redeemed your people,
the descendants of Jacob and Joseph.

The waters saw you, God,
the waters saw you and writhed;
the very depths were convulsed.
The clouds poured down water,
the heavens resounded with thunder;
your arrows flashed back and forth.
Your thunder was heard in the whirlwind,
your lightning lit up the world;
the earth trembled and quaked.
Your path led through the sea,
your way through the mighty waters,
though your footprints were not seen.

You led your people like a flock
by the hand of Moses and Aaron.

Let that be your rhythm. Cry out. Remember. Meditate. Declare.

In your own way. At your own time. What are you holding in that would be better released, cried out, let go?

Remembering, thinking back, thinking about, revisiting, recalling, releasing. What do you need to remember so you can become better aware of your true self? What good stories from your past can help you grasp the reality of the present? The Psalmist thought back, reviewed, and rejoiced at what the Lord had done.

Meditate on who God is and what He has done. Declare it. Dwell on the large, the better, the grace, the hope, the assurance, the healing. State it. Announce it. Proclaim it.

The season you are enduring might not feel like reclining in a comfortable chair. But it is time with the Comforter amid the uncomfortable realities. You are growing, developing, being transformed.

Maybe contentment isn't the absence of trouble. Maybe it's the quiet decision to keep trusting through it

Medical and Psychological Benefits of Contentment

1. Reduced Stress and Anxiety: Contentment lowers levels of the stress hormone cortisol, reducing the risk of stress-related illnesses such as hypertension, heart disease, and immune dysfunction.
2. Improved Mental Health: Contentment is associated with higher levels of serotonin and dopamine, improving mood and reducing symptoms of depression and anxiety.
3. Better Sleep: A content and peaceful mindset helps achieve better sleep quality, which is essential for overall health.
4. Increased Longevity: Studies suggest that people who practice gratitude and contentment tend to live longer, healthier lives due to reduced stress and improved emotional regulation.
5. Stronger Relationships: Content individuals are often less envious or competitive, fostering healthier and more fulfilling interpersonal relationships.
6. Greater Resilience: Contentment promotes a mindset of gratitude, helping individuals navigate challenges with a positive outlook.
7. Improved Physical Health: Contentment is linked to lower blood pressure, a healthier immune system, and decreased risk of chronic diseases.

By cultivating contentment, one can achieve a holistic sense of well-being that positively impacts both the mind and body.

11 FAITHFUL IN THE SMALL THINGS

"Contentment comes in considering others above ourselves and giving ourselves to serve them." —**William B. Barcley**[13]

Few people knew her publicly. But her quiet phone calls brought peace to friends who felt forgotten. Her whispered prayers in a small house in a small town carried more weight than she realized. Her smile—seen by only a handful—brought hope to each one.

He worked at a grocery store bagging milk, cereal, ice cream, chewing gum. Customers hurried through the checkout line, rarely learning his name. Many held bigger titles, larger salaries, fuller resumes. But this man? He found joy in serving—content in doing the unnoticed work that mattered.

The pastor of a tiny church. Parents quietly caring for their son with special needs. A businessman stepping into retirement with less money than experts advised—but more peace than he'd ever known.

What we call small might be sacred in God's economy.

We want to do big things. We want to be part of something that matters. But somewhere along the way, "big" started to mean "seen."

And we began to overlook the small.

13 William B. Barcley, *The Secret of Contentment* (Phillipsburg, NJ: P&R Publishing, 2010), 149.

We've been trained to count.

Count heads in the room. Count dollars in the bank. Count followers, likes, scores, stats. Count books sold. Sermons preached. Hands raised. Buildings built. Crowds gathered.

And when the numbers aren't high, we feel low. Defeated. Useless. Unimportant. Of little value.

We assume something's wrong with us. We question our worth, our calling, our direction. We compare our invisible to someone else's viral. We scroll through highlight reels, all while hiding our own reality.

But what if we're counting the wrong things?

What if value is found not in how many, but in who? Not in how much, but in how deep? Not in the scoreboard, but in the stories?

Jesus knew how to gather crowds.

But He often walked away from them.

He noticed one in a tree. He knelt beside one caught in shame. He paused to bless the children others pushed away. He dined with outsiders. He wept with those grieving. He washed feet. He listened. He asked questions. He told stories.

No stat sheet promotes those types of moments.

But God noticed. And God notices.

Those He loved and invited and welcomed noticed.

And we—chasing crowds, craving applause, counting followers—are invited into a different way.

To mentor a few, not manage a multitude. To shepherd a flock, not perform for a stadium. To linger in a conversation instead of rushing to another obligation.

We're tempted to believe we haven't done enough if we can't show impressive numbers. But maybe the quiet prayer, the anonymous kindness, the faithful presence are the truest victories.

So today, let's wave goodbye. Goodbye to the pressure, the performance, the pursuit of popularity.

Let's choose contentment. Let's measure success in hugs, not headlines. In faithfulness, not fame. In depth, not digits.

Because maybe small isn't less. Maybe small is sacred. Maybe small is where Jesus still shows up, unnoticed by the crowd but fully present to the few who see Him in every little thing.

A few years ago, I became aware of my need for a better balance between my mental and spiritual lives and my responsibilities. So that became my word for the year: balance. I eventually wrote about how that word is healthy for all of us. My book, *Equilibrium: 31 Ways to Stay Balanced on Life's Uneven Surfaces*, is what I still hope to apply.

Why am I bringing it up here? Because of the first two chapters of *Equilibrium*. Chapter One: Believe in the Big and Chapter Two: Be Faithful in the Little. And that is where we are in *Contentment*. Yes, believe in what seems impossible. Yes, pray prayers that will need miracles to become realities. Yes, set outrageous goals. But as you are believing in the big, be faithful in the tiny, the small, the no-one-will-ever-know-it-was-me, the everyday, the here, the now, the silent.

An opportunity awaits us, even when no applause will ever hit the soundwaves. Faithful, that is the word. Faithful in the little, that is the goal. If we choose to live that way and love that way, we might find a better-balanced view of life and this world might become better because of us.

> *Believe in the big. That miracle which might come. That impossible which might happen. That dream which might just be waiting on you to resurrect it. And, while believing and hoping and pursuing, let us not miss this moment. Each word has value. Every meal has value. Every second of every hour of every day of every week of every month of every year—find balance in each moment.* [14]

---

14 Chris Maxwell, *Equilibrium: 31 Ways to Stay Balanced on Life's Uneven Surface* (Travelers Rest, SC: True Potential, Inc., 2022), 25.

- *Things that seem small to us might be the most important things in the world....*
- *Things no one will notice are noticed by the One that really matters....*
- *Things are right there waiting for us to do them.*[15]

God's Kingdom Measures Differently

Jesus told stories about mustard seeds, lost coins, and widows giving pennies. He saw people others ignored. He celebrated actions that never went viral.

The greatest in His kingdom? Servants. The ones who wash feet. The ones who stay behind the scenes. The ones who show up, again and again, without needing a spotlight.

What we often overlook, heaven applauds.

The Work That Doesn't Seem to Matter

Folding the laundry. Sending the text. Writing the lesson. Encouraging your team even when morale is low. Leading worship for fifteen people. Praying for your child one more time. Smiling at your neighbor when you'd rather stay hidden.

None of it is wasted.

None of it.

It might not feel impressive, but it is impactful.

The Discipline of Showing Up

Contentment often looks like ordinary obedience. Not chasing a platform. Not proving your worth. Just being faithful in the assignment God has given today.

Not because it's glamorous.

But because it's good.

---

15 Maxwell, *Equilibrium*, 24.

In those small acts of faithfulness, we're being formed. Not into famous people. But into faithful ones.

Small Is Where We Start—and Often Stay

Maybe your work doesn't get noticed. Maybe your church isn't large. Maybe your business didn't grow like you hoped. Maybe your progress feels painfully slow.

But you are being faithful.

And in God's kingdom, that's more than enough.

Faithfulness is success. Obedience is significance. Small things, done with great love, make heaven smile.

The woman who whispers prayers in her kitchen and dials the phone to comfort a friend. The man bagging milk and cereal with a quiet smile for strangers who will never know his name. The parents rocking their son through another restless night, loving him in silence. The pastor preaching hope to fifteen people in a drafty sanctuary.

These are the stories heaven celebrates.

And yours is one of them.

So, keep going. Keep showing up. Keep tending what's been placed in your hands.

Contentment grows best when we embrace the sacredness of the small.

Living Out Contentment: A Personal Invitation

Contentment isn't just an idea—it's a practice. A way of noticing beauty, receiving grace, and choosing presence. One of the most powerful ways to cultivate a life of contentment is by doing the things that help you slow down, breathe deep, and smile from the inside out.

Here's a list of things that help me live that way. Not to impress anyone. Not to escape reality. But to lean into a deeper kind of peace—by doing things I actually enjoy:

- Walking to a waterfall and staring at its beauty. Standing still and letting wonder speak louder than worry.
- Going to a baseball game. The rhythm of innings, the sound of the crowd, the space to just be.
- Flying on a plane. Not because travel is easy, but because something about the sky reminds me how big life is—and how small my stress can feel from up there.
- Reading a book. Letting words take me somewhere deeper than distraction.
- Shooting free throws when no one is watching. A quiet rhythm. A practice in solitude. A moment that belongs to no one else.
- Listening to my favorite songs. Not for noise, but for soul connection. For memories. For melody and meaning.
- Eating out. Good food. Good conversation. A space I don't have to clean up.
- Writing a journal entry. Not to be profound—just to be honest. To empty and to notice. To remember.
- Spending time with dear friends. The kind of time that doesn't need a filter or a performance.

Here are a few more that speak to my soul:

- Sitting in silence with no agenda.
- Watching the sky change colors at dusk.
- Sending an unexpected note of encouragement.
- Laughing with someone who gets me.
- Letting go of my to-do list, just for today.

Now it's your turn.

Take out a piece of paper. Open a note on your phone. Write your own list of things that bring you peace, joy, and grounding. Things that help you be present. Things that whisper, "This is enough."

Now—do them.

This is how we live a life of contentment. Not by chasing more. But by receiving what already surrounds us. By saying yes to the simple, sacred joys we often overlook.

12

RECEIVING WHAT IS

"We don't have to wait to feel content before we approach God; neither do we need to beat ourselves up for not feeling content yet. These things take time, and God has time." **—Tanya Marlowk**[16]

The storm had knocked trees down across the road. Huge branches sprawled across our neighbor's yard, blocking the main street—the one I always took to church. The familiar path was gone. Closed. Obstructed. Inaccessible.

I slowed to a stop, unsure of what to do.

Then a police officer waved me down. He didn't shout instructions or argue with the trees. He simply pointed toward the grass—across a yard I'd never driven through before.

"That's the way out now," he said. "Your only way out."

It wasn't the road. It wasn't paved. It wasn't what I was used to. But it was the only way through.

I turned off the road and onto the grass. What felt unfamiliar became freeing. What looked inconvenient became possible.

16 Tanya Marlow in Jennie Pollock, *If Only: Finding Joyful Contentment in the Face of Lack and Longing* (Epsom, Surrey, England: The Good Book Company, 2020), 111.

And it got me where I needed to go.

Life is often like that.

We set out expecting smooth streets and clear signs, but then the unexpected falls across our plans. A storm of disappointment. A tree of grief. A blocked road of unmet expectations. We're stuck at a standstill, staring at what should've been.

And that's where the invitation comes: Don't resist reality. Don't deny what's happened. Instead, receive what is.

It's the first step toward contentment.

From Now On

The Apostle Paul knew what it felt like to live a life shaped by expectations—his own and everyone else's. In his world, performance mattered. Obedience to the law earned you status. External signs like circumcision served as proof that you belonged.

But then Jesus disrupted all of that.

Paul writes to the Galatians: "May I never boast except in the cross of our Lord Jesus Christ, through which the world has been crucified to me, and I to the world" (6:14).

Everything Paul used to rely on—status, heritage, control—was like a well-paved road that no longer led anywhere. The cross had redefined his direction. A spiritual conversation made it a reality. And from that moment on, he didn't boast in his religious performance. He didn't try to earn God's approval. He simply received it.

He received what is.

A Yard, Not a Street

Paul didn't say that the road to contentment was easy. He said it was different.

"What counts is the new creation." (v. 15)

Not how religious you appear. Not whether others approve. Not the perfect plan you mapped out.

What counts is what God has already done in you.

The path may feel like a yard, not a street. It may feel like grass under your tires and uncertainty under your feet. But it's grace. And it's enough.

Bearing the Marks

Paul goes on to say something striking: "From now on, let no one cause me trouble, for I bear on my body the marks of Jesus" (v. 17).

The word, "marks," refers to scars—real ones. Paul had suffered for Christ. He had been beaten and rejected. He wasn't pretending. He wasn't polishing up his life for others. He had received what was—suffering included—and found something more solid than comfort: purpose.

From now on, he was done with people-pleasing. From now on, he was finished with performance. From now on, he walked in freedom.

Contentment Begins Here

We often think contentment comes when everything is just right. When the roads are clear. When the skies are blue. When the world cooperates with our plans.

But Paul shows us another way: contentment comes when we let go of what we thought life would be and receive what is already ours in Christ.

Grace.

Peace.

Mercy.

A new creation.

It's not about finding a perfect road—it's about following Jesus through the grass.

A Few Questions

- What road were you expecting life to follow? How has that changed?
- What are you trying to control that God is asking you to receive?
- How might your day change if you let go of what "should be" and received what is?

A Few Words to Hold on To

"What counts is the new creation" (Galatians 6:15).

"From now on, let no one cause me trouble, for I bear on my body the marks of Jesus" (Galatians 6:17).

"The grace of our Lord Jesus Christ be with your spirit, brothers and sisters. Amen" (Galatians 6:18).

A Gentle Reminder

The road may look unfamiliar. The path may be softer, less traveled, less expected. But there is grace here. There is peace here. There is Jesus here.

From now on, you don't have to earn it. From now on, you don't have to force it. From now on, you can simply receive what is.

And that may be the first step toward the contentment you've been longing for all along.

Contentment comes when we stop resisting reality and start receiving it.

We are often taught to fight, fix, or flee anything unpleasant. But contentment doesn't come from constant striving—it comes from a posture of reception. That doesn't mean we surrender to passivity. It means we stop pretending, stop comparing, stop trying to rearrange the universe to suit our plans.

Contentment begins when we learn to receive what is, even if it's not what we wanted.

We receive what is with open hands, not clenched fists. With grace instead of bitterness. With hope rather than fear. We receive our lives—their beauty and their brokenness—as gifts. Not always gifts we asked for, but gifts, nonetheless.

Take inventory:

- What am I resisting right now that I might need to receive?
- What disappointment, diagnosis, or detour have I been fighting that might be reshaped in the hands of God?
- What might happen if I open my hands instead of raising my fists?

Grace for the Present Moment

Sometimes receiving means letting go of what could've been, what used to be, or what should have happened. We find grace in the present moment—not the perfect moment, but the real one.

We breathe. We pause. We whisper, "This is the life I've been given today, and I will receive it with open hands."

An Unlikely Prayer

We can borrow the prayer from the ancient follower of Jesus who wrote, "I have learned to be content whatever the circumstances" (Philippians 4:11). That line—written from a prison cell—reminds us that contentment is not circumstantial. It is spiritual. It is not found in control, but in surrender.

We don't have to like everything we receive. But we can still find contentment in the receiving.

We can still say, "This is hard. And this is holy." "This hurts. And this is part of my story." "This is not what I wanted. And God is still present."

Closing Invitation

Don't miss what is because you're waiting on what isn't.

Let the life you have become the life you live. Let the day you've been given become the day you honor. Even if trees are blocking your street.

Even if you need to drive on the grass.

Receive what is. It's the only way to find contentment in a world that keeps shouting for more.

What is God the Father Saying About Contentment?

The Father, creator of the universe, speaks through His creation, whispering contentment into every sunrise and sunset. He says, "Be still, and know that I am God" (Psalm 46:10). Contentment is not about having everything but about knowing Him who holds everything.

The Father invites us to trust His providence, reminding us that we are His children; orphans adopted by God. He says, "I know the plans I have for you ... plans to give you hope and a future" (Jeremiah 29:11). When life feels uncertain, the Father's voice steadies us: "My grace is sufficient for you" (2 Corinthians 12:9). Contentment begins with resting in the Father's love, knowing He is working all things together for good.

What is Jesus the Mentor and Savior Saying About Contentment?

Jesus lived contentment. He walked dusty roads, slept under stars, and loved deeply without needing applause. His words echo through the Sermon on the Mount: "Do not worry about your life.... But seek first His kingdom and His righteousness" (see Matthew 6:25–33). Jesus, our mentor, teaches us that contentment isn't found in more but in less—less striving, less comparison, less fear.

His life demonstrates simplicity and surrender, reminding us that we can have peace even in storms. As Savior, He says, "Come to me, all who are weary and burdened, and I will give you rest" (Matthew 11:28). Contentment is found at His feet, where we trade our chaos for His calm, our burdens for His freedom.

What is the Wind of God Saying About Contentment?

The Spirit, the Wind of God, breathes contentment into our restless souls. He whispers when we're overwhelmed: "You are not alone; I am with you" (see John 14:16–17). The Spirit convicts us of the idols we chase—success, approval, possessions—and draws us back to the heart of God.

He empowers us to live counterculturally, producing the fruit of peace and joy in a world of hurry and hustle. The Spirit says, "Wait for the Lord; be strong and take heart and wait for the Lord" (Psalm 27:14). He invites us to trust the unseen, to rest in God's timing, and to find contentment in His presence, even when the world offers none.

INTERLUDE: FINDING STILLNESS IN THE ORDINARY

> *"Contentment, however, encourages you to walk. To take it easy. To trust that your needs will be met and your life will be full of joy."* —**Rachel Cruze**[17]

There are days when contentment feels like a foreign language.

You want to believe what you've read. You want to receive every sentence on these pages. You want to live a life grounded, rooted, centered. But then life happens. Medical bills come in. Dreams get delayed. You scroll past another story of someone doing more, being more, achieving more.

And you feel less.

You look at your life—your friends who aren't responding, your business that's barely surviving, your body that isn't cooperating, your past that still lingers—and contentment feels like a word for other people. Not for you. Not here.

You wonder if you're falling behind. You wonder if you're too late, too small, too flawed. You wonder if the best version of life just skipped over your address.

17 Rachel Cruze, *The Contentment Journal* (Mahwah, NJ: Ramsey Press, 2019).

And yet, even here, contentment whispers an invitation.

It's not the shout of the world demanding results. It's not the applause of success or the voice of perfection. It's quieter than that. More honest. More human.

It says you're still loved.

It says you're not forgotten.

It says there's life right here—in this version of your story.

You are not your metrics. You are not your numbers, your earnings, your standing, your title, your likes, your latest. You are more than the version of yourself that you compare to others.

The practices of contentment aren't flashy. They aren't impressive. But they are faithful.

They're found in the early mornings, the uncelebrated moments, the unnoticed acts of peace. They are practiced, not performed. Lived, not posted. Embraced, not earned.

You will still wrestle. You will still feel loss. You will still limp. You will still wonder if you're enough.

You are.

Not because of what you've done.

But because of who you are.

Because of *whose* you are.

Now—let's take a step. Not toward striving but toward stillness. Not toward perfection but toward peace.

Let's practice contentment together.

The Sacred Pause: Choosing Contentment in a Restless World

Contentment whispers to us, but we rarely stop long enough to listen. It invites us to slow down, take a breath, and trust that the world will keep spinning even if we step away. Yet we resist. We fill our calendars, push through exhaustion, and convince ourselves that rest is a luxury we cannot afford.

But what if the rest we avoid is exactly what we need to rediscover contentment?

The Power of a Nap

It feels almost absurd to suggest it: taking a nap as a spiritual practice. But the Psalmist understood the connection between rest and trust. In Psalm 4:8, David prayed, "In peace I will lie down and sleep, for you alone, LORD, make me dwell in safety."

A nap isn't just about recharging our bodies; it's about surrendering our constant striving. It's an act of trust that God can handle the world without us for a little while. When we rest, we remind our overworked minds and weary hearts that our worth isn't tied to productivity.

Try it. Turn off the phone, find a quiet corner, and close your eyes. Whisper a prayer before you drift off: "Lord, teach me to rest in You."

Selecting Time Off

Pastors often talk about Sabbath but rarely live it. We encourage our congregations to rest while working through our own supposed "day off." But contentment demands boundaries. Choosing time off—real, uninterrupted time—isn't selfish; it's biblical.

Psalm 23 reminds us that the Good Shepherd "makes me lie down in green pastures" (v. 2). He knows we won't rest unless He leads us there. And in those green pastures, away from the demands of life, we notice the beauty of God's creation. We hear His voice more clearly.

Block out a day on your calendar. No meetings. No emails. Spend it with your family, take a walk, or sit with your Bible under an open sky.

Noticing the Wonder All Around

Contentment often hides in the ordinary moments we overlook. The morning dew sparkling in the sunlight. The laughter of a child. The aroma of freshly brewed coffee. These small wonders are gifts from God, invitations to slow down and savor the goodness of life.

Psalm 19:1 declares, "The heavens declare the glory of God; the skies proclaim the work of his hands." Creation sings of God's greatness, but we miss the song because we're too busy to listen.

Pause today. Look around. What do you see? What do you hear? What smells, sounds, or sights remind you of God's love? These moments of wonder are reminders that contentment isn't found in more—it's found in noticing what we already have.

Rewiring the Mind

Our minds are wired for negativity. We dwell on what's wrong, replay failures, and anticipate the worst. But Scripture offers a better way. Romans 12:2 urges us to "be transformed by the renewing of your mind." Contentment begins when we train our brains to think differently.

The Psalms provide a roadmap. In Psalm 42:5, the writer speaks to his own soul: "Why, my soul, are you downcast? Why so disturbed within me? Put your hope in God." It's a reminder that we have the power to redirect our thoughts.

Start small. When discontent creeps in, pause and pray. Recite verses like Psalm 46:10: "Be still, and know that I am God." Create a habit of listing blessings every morning. Over time these practices reshape our neurological pathways, creating space for peace and gratitude.

A Closing Thought

Contentment isn't a place we arrive at; it's a rhythm we choose daily. It's found in the simplicity of a nap, the discipline of time off, the beauty of ordinary moments, and the rewiring of our minds to see God's goodness all around us.

Today, let's choose contentment. Let's rest in the truth of Psalm 34:8: "Taste and see that the LORD is good." Let's taste, see, and believe that His goodness is enough. And in the sacred pause, may we find the peace we've been searching for all along.

SECTION THREE

MOVING TOWARD GRATITUDE AND GENEROSITY

13

WAKING UP GRATEFUL

"Contentment is simple, but it isn't easy." **—Megan Hill**[18]

Do you wake up early each morning? Or sleep in as long as possible?

Some minds start fast. Some need time. Some rise with a list. Others rise with a sigh. Some need coffee. And more coffee. And maybe still more coffee.

Some of us wake with words ready—to write, to pray, to read, to reflect. Others wake with worries waiting.

But whatever your wake-up routine—whatever your mood, your method, your menu—those first few moments matter more than you realize. They are sacred spaces. Blessed beginnings. The doorway into your day.

And those first thoughts? They don't always arrive with gratitude. Sometimes they bring stress, dread, or distractions. That's why we must train the mind early. Change the station. Choose the story. Turn the channel.

Because contentment often begins before breakfast. Gratitude is grown in the early hours.

---

18 Megan Hill, *Contentment: Seeing God's Goodness* (Phillipsburg, NJ: P&R Publishing, 2018), 11.

It doesn't depend on the mood we wake up with—but on the direction we decide to go.

The first few minutes of your day shape so much more than just your mood. They inform your mindset, your focus, your pace. And often, without meaning to, we wake up into worry. Into rushing. Into comparison. Into noise.

But what if we woke up with gratitude?

What if contentment began before the day ever really started?

That isn't just an idea—it's a practice. A rhythm. A spiritual decision to begin the day with thanks instead of lack.

From Complaining to Contentment

It's tempting to start each morning thinking about what you don't have:

- Not enough time
- Not enough energy
- Not enough help
- Not enough success
- Not enough sleep

But contentment invites a different voice.

It doesn't ignore pain or pretend everything is perfect. It simply looks for goodness first. Gratitude doesn't erase hardship—but it realigns your soul.

Paul would love to voice our wakeup call with these words:

"Give thanks in all circumstances; for this is God's will for you in Christ Jesus" (1 Thessalonians 5:18).

It's not about giving thanks for everything. It's about giving thanks in everything.

Even on a tired Tuesday. Even when the week has already gone sideways. Even when the mirror, the inbox, and the calendar feel heavy.

The Story of a Morning Prayer

There's a scene in Scripture where David, overwhelmed and under attack, makes a morning choice:

> *"In the morning, LORD, you hear my voice;*
>
> *in the morning I lay my requests before you and wait expectantly"* (Psalm 5:3).

David doesn't start the day by fixing his problems. He starts by praying. By placing his heart before God. By waiting—not with dread, but with expectation.

It's a picture of contentment in the chaos. A choice to bring it all before God. A way to wake up differently.

The Practice: Waking Up Grateful

Let's try it.

Before you reach for your phone. Before the news, the noise, the to-do list. Pause. Pray. Give thanks.

Here are a few first steps:

- Keep a thankfulness journal by your bed.
- Write three specific things each morning that you're thankful for. Don't repeat. Make it fresh. Let it stretch you.
- Pray with your eyes still closed.
- Begin with this simple prayer: "God, thank You for this day. Thank You that I'm alive. Thank You that You are with me."
- Read a Scripture before anything else.
- Try Psalm 23, Matthew 6:25–34, or Philippians 4:4–9. Let your thoughts anchor there.
- Resist the urge to scroll.
- Don't let the first voice of your day be social media or the headlines. Protect those first five minutes.

Contentment Grows in the Morning

Each morning is a chance to start again—not just physically, but spiritually. Not every morning will feel magical. But each one holds potential.

The act of waking up with gratitude is not about pretending everything is fine.

It's about remembering who you are.

Remembering who God is.

Remembering what's still good.

Suggestions for Contentment Through the Day

Morning: The morning is a gift, a fresh start, a blank canvas waiting for grace to paint its strokes. Mornings are for meeting the Maker before meeting the world. Begin the day with prayer, gratitude, and silence. Let contentment rise with the sun as you acknowledge that God's mercies are new every morning.

Afternoon: By midday, the demands of the day can feel overwhelming. Pause. Afternoons need a moment of stillness—a deep breath to reset the soul. Find time to reflect, even briefly, on God's provision and faithfulness. A walk, a quiet prayer, a short nap, or simply looking up at the sky can restore contentment in the middle of busyness.

Evening: Evening is for exhaling, for letting go of what didn't happen and thanking God for what did. The day ends better when we release its weight into God's hands. Finish with prayer, laughter, or reflection. Contentment comes in trusting that even while you sleep, God is at work, and His love sustains you.

These rhythms of the day gently encourage us to choose contentment. Not as a fleeting emotion but as a steady, Spirit-led posture of the heart.

The Healing Power of Hope

Contentment doesn't mean settling. It doesn't mean we stop dreaming or striving. Instead, it's about finding hope and healing along the way, during each day.

I often think of Jesus' words in Matthew 11:28–30: "Come to me, all you who are weary and burdened, and I will give you rest." That's where contentment lives—not in achieving or arriving, but in the rest He offers right now.

Hope grows when we choose to believe that today, this day, matters. Healing happens when we accept that even in our imperfections, God is doing something beautiful. And that contentment is found not in what we hold in our hands but in the peace we carry in our hearts.

What gifts have you overlooked today? What moments are waiting for you to unwrap? They are there—hidden in the ordinary, full of grace. They are your invitation to contentment, to healing, to hope.

I remember a day like that, a day when life seemed to slow down.

How did it begin? With this: I wasn't in a hurry that day.

It was rare for me then—my life, once filled with the rush of schedules and tasks, was in the process of learning to slow down. I was sitting outside watching the leaves fall, one by one. The breeze carried them gently to the ground as if whispering, "This is how life should be."

I thought about the life I used to live before my brain injury—fast-paced, high-energy, always striving for the next thing. That life seemed like a distant memory, but in this slower rhythm I began to notice what I had overlooked.

A child laughed in the distance. A bird paused on a branch. The clouds moved effortlessly across the sky.

I felt a quiet contentment settle into my soul, not because everything was perfect but because I was present enough to see what had always been there.

The Scar That Speaks

Someone recently asked me about a scar. It was there, carved into me, and that person seemed to see it for the first time.

Scars in life come. Because of various reasons, they arrive. And they stay.

But over time, scars can begin to teach us something new.

"Chris," it seemed to say, "you're still here."

The scar was no longer a symbol of loss. It was a sign of survival. It reminded me of the strength I didn't know I had and the grace I didn't deserve but still received.

Contentment isn't about erasing a scar or pretending pain didn't happen. It is about learning to see the beauty in the healing, however imperfect it looks.

How do we learn it better? How do we live it better?

Begin with gratefulness. Early in the day. At noon. In the evening. When we wake and before we go to sleep. Prior to conversations and duties, and after them. Thankful for today, for life, for now. Making the choice to rejoice.

However and whenever you wake up, whatever you do early in the day, welcome gratefulness. It can stay with you all day.

14 RESTING WITHOUT EARNING

"Even the seemingly passive activity of a good night's sleep is a gift from the Lord!" **—Megan Hill**[19]

The man leaned against the breakroom wall, wiping sweat from his forehead. His English was broken but his meaning was clear.

"Your culture," he said, shaking his head slowly, "it ... ruins me. No nap."

He laughed, but it wasn't just a joke. Back home in Mexico, afternoons meant pausing. Work stopped, bodies rested, conversations slowed. Here, rest felt like weakness. Here, if you closed your eyes after lunch people wondered if you were lazy.

"I need nap," he said again, half-smiling, half-pleading. "But ... no nap here."

His words followed me home. I kept thinking about them later that afternoon, later that week.

When did we decide exhaustion was the goal? When did rest become something we have to earn?

---

19 Megan Hill, *Contentment: Seeing God's Goodness* (Phillipsburg, NJ: P&R Publishing, 2018), 35.

Maybe he's right. Maybe we've forgotten something simple. Somewhere along the way, we traded quiet afternoons for endless hustle. We replaced pauses with productivity, naps with notifications. We forgot how to rest.

No confirmation is needed to prove that the price has been paid when we enter a place of rest. We aren't required to submit a proposal on the new day's agenda before we can peacefully, calmly wake up and enter a new day smiling. We shouldn't state a long list of tasks completed before we stop for lunch break. We don't need to show how much we accomplished during a day before we fall asleep at night. We must not allow our brains to continue driving frantically in the fast lane while we desperately need to pull over and fall asleep at night.

We should rest. Regularly. Without a sense of earning. Without proof of our value. Intentionally taking time to rest.

We know that, don't we? But why don't we rest as we know we should?

In today's world, productivity has become a measurement of worth. We're praised for how much we hustle, how long we grind, how often we sacrifice. We wear busyness like a badge, but deep down, we're breaking.

So many of us only feel permission to rest after we've earned it.

But what if rest isn't a reward?

What if rest is a calling?

What if, instead of waiting until we're exhausted and empty, we built rest into the rhythm of our lives—on purpose, with intention, and without guilt?

Living this way, the resting-without-earning-way, requires something deeper than permission. It requires trust.

I've met people whose lives preach louder than any sermon. They don't use big words. They don't need the spotlight. But they walk with a quiet confidence that comes from somewhere deeper.

Not because everything is certain. But because they've learned to trust—especially when it's not.

Their faith isn't polished. What makes it real? It's weathered.

I want to be more like them. I want to believe more like how they believe.

Remember this: No one gets to faith easily. It usually comes with scars. We've all fallen. We've all asked, "What if I jump and no one catches me? What if I trust and things get worse?"

Even the faithful weren't fearless. Abraham left without knowing where he was going.

Sarah laughed when hearing of a promise to come.

They didn't believe because they were strong. They believed because they saw something we often miss:

God is the builder.

God is the architect.

God is the promise keeper.

That's what Hebrews 11 tells us. Not that faith is easy. But that it's possible.

We Are Surrounded

Picture the race. The track stretching farther than your eyes can see.

And you—not standing alone, not striving alone.

Hebrews 11 reminds us of those who lived by faith. They didn't always see the results. They didn't finish with medals or applause. But they believed. They trusted. They ran their race.

And we are surrounded by that great cloud of witnesses. Their lives whisper the same truth: God is faithful. Keep going. Lay down what weighs you down. Run light. Run free.

Not to prove your worth. Not to earn applause. But because the race has already been marked out for you. Because Jesus has already run ahead of you. Because He is *"the pioneer and perfecter of faith"* (Hebrews 12:2).

The finish line is not your achievement. The finish line is Him.

That's contentment.

Not running to prove, but running to trust.

Not running alone, but surrounded.

Not running empty, but strengthened by Jesus Himself.

We live in a world that prizes results. Show me the outcome. Prove your worth. Perform.

Faith flips that script.

It whispers, "You don't have to see it all. You don't have to know every detail. You don't have to be perfect. You just must trust the One who does."

> *"Faith is confidence in what we hope for and assurance about what we do not see."* (Hebrews 11:1)

Confidence and contentment aren't opposites. They're companions.

To rest is to believe God is still at work even when I am not. To trust is to admit I don't have to figure everything out. To have faith is to find peace—even with unanswered questions.

And that's when we begin to see like the saints who came before us. Not with natural eyes. But with the lens of promise.

It's like the photographer adjusting her lens—blurring the background, zooming in on what matters.

Faith focuses on what lasts. It narrows in on God's voice, God's future, God's yes.

Others may only see confusion. But people of faith see what's coming.

They live not just in the moment—but in the assurance of what's still ahead.

They were looking for a better destination. Not just a better job or house or reputation. They longed for home—and they knew this world wasn't it.

So they kept walking. They kept waiting. They kept trusting.

And God was not ashamed to be called their God (see Hebrews 11:16).

I want to live that way. I want to see that way. Not with anxious eyes scanning for results. But with content eyes resting in God's goodness—even in the not-yet.

I'm learning to say:

"I don't know how this ends, but I know Who walks with me."

"I don't see the full picture, but I trust the hands that are painting it."

"I don't have all the answers, but I'm not alone in the questions."

Those aren't just religious cliches. They are confessions of faith.

And faith is enough.

I wonder if my friend's still taking those naps. If he's still fighting off the pressure to prove himself every hour of every day.

I hope so. I hope he's found the quiet gift we're all searching for.

Maybe we all need to remember what he reminded me: Rest isn't something to earn. It's something to receive.

A Biblical Invitation to Rest

We forget that God Himself rested. After creation, when all was finished, He stopped—not because He was tired, but to model something for us.

> *"By the seventh day God had finished the work he had been doing; so on the seventh day he rested from all his work."* (Genesis 2:2)

Later, He invites His people to do the same—not just as a suggestion, but as a command. To set aside a day. To resist striving. To remember they are more than their labor.

And then Jesus comes, extending the same invitation:

> *"Come to me, all you who are weary and burdened, and I will give you rest."* (Matthew 11:28)

He doesn't say, "Come to me after you've fixed it all." He doesn't say, "Come to me when your to-do list is done." He simply says, "Come."

Rest That Leads to Contentment

Rest and contentment are closely connected. Rest recalibrates the soul. It reminds us that our value isn't in our output.

Some of the most contented people are those who know how to rest well:

- They pause before they're forced to.
- They schedule solitude.
- They take walks without multitasking.
- They nap without guilt.
- They know when to say no—even to good things.

Rest is a way of saying, "I trust that the world will keep spinning without me. I trust that God is still in control. I trust that I don't have to prove my worth every hour of the day."

The Practice: Resting on Purpose

If you want to grow in contentment, you'll need to grow in rest.

A few intentional steps:

- Establish a weekly rhythm of rest.
- Pick one day—or even one afternoon—each week where you intentionally do less. No working. No striving. Just breathing, being, delighting in what's good.

- Practice micro-pauses throughout the day.
- Step outside. Stretch. Breathe deeply for sixty seconds. These short resets help reframe your day.
- Let go of guilt.
- When you hear the voice that says, "You should be doing more," pause and replace it with, "God invites me to rest."
- Celebrate small.
- Sit on the porch. Drink some water. Listen to music. Watch a sunset. Don't rush through the moments that restore you.

Sabbath and Soulfulness

Sabbath isn't just an Old Testament command—it's a New Testament lifestyle. It's a resistance to hurry. A way of saying that grace is enough.

Contentment doesn't grow in burnout. It grows in margin.

Sometimes, the most spiritual thing you can do is take a nap.

Or say no.

Or step away from the noise.

Or turn off your phone.

Or take a walk just to breathe.

Having Breakfast with Jesus

Imagining I was having breakfast with Jesus changed the way I view mornings.

I've written similar stories like this in two of my books. I've written journal entries often, imagining sitting beside Jesus and eating a meal with him. But this time? It was different. It is different.

Not the busy mornings filled with working while eating my breakfast cereal. Not the sleepy ones where prayer feels distant or forgotten. But a quiet morning. A still morning. The kind of morning where the fog still rests on the water and silence says more than noise.

In my imagination, I wake and walk toward a kitchen. Jesus is there, the risen One, and He's not preaching a sermon or working a miracle. He's waiting—with breakfast. Somehow the food is also there—complete, perfect, like everything He does. And it isn't fish for me. He knows I don't like seafood. I'm not like Peter. In that way, at least.

Instead, Jesus thought of me. Really thought of me. He's got scrambled eggs and grits, wheat toast with strawberry jelly, and He hands me a glass of orange juice, cold and comforting. He smiles like He's waited forever for this moment.

"Come," He says, "eat breakfast."

The invitation moves something deep in me.

He doesn't bring up the past, though He could. He doesn't list my failures, though I remember so many. He simply calls me close and offers food.

I sit near Him.

I wonder why He is here, of all places. And why He cooks breakfast for me, of all people. I look down at my plate, then up at His face. He looks at me—not through me—and says, "This is where new mornings begin. Right here. With Me."

He asks the question I hoped He wouldn't: "Do you love Me?"

I nod, trying to convince myself as much as Him. "Yes, Lord."

He asks again.

And again.

And something deep within me breaks free. He's not testing me. He's healing me. Rewriting shame into purpose.

Then He leans in and says the thing that stays with me long after the breakfast is done: "Feed My sheep. Not just with sermons or strategies, but with kindness, presence, conversation, meals, honesty, and grace. Go where they are. Bring My love with you. Serve my love to everyone you meet."

I begin to see it more clearly. Making disciples isn't just about teaching. It's about knowing the feel of their hunger. It's about sitting down before standing up. It's about offering what they'll receive, not forcing what they fear.

Jesus isn't asking me to impress. He's asking me to follow. To walk behind Him, step by step, so others can see the trail He's already blazed.

"Follow Me," He says one more time.

And I do.

Not because I have it all figured out, but because breakfast with Jesus changes everything.

Stories like that can remind us about the illusion of always producing. Always succeeding. Always advancing. Always learning to pause without guilt.

Follow Jesus. To His miracles and His teachings and His long walks and His stories and His death and His resurrection. And also to His naps and His time away, alone, just with the Father.

Maybe the miracle we need most to see Jesus do for us is to help us stop being so busy trying to craft our own miracle.

Maybe the miracle we need most to see Jesus do for us is to teach us to stop. Just stop.

Spiritual Health

Spiritual health is strongly associated with quality of life and mental health. Studies have shown that individuals with higher spiritual health experience better mental health and adapt to stress more successfully. For instance, spiritual health has been linked to lower levels of depressive symptoms and anxiety.

Finding True Contentment

Practice Gratitude. Write down three things you're grateful for each day. Gratitude shifts our focus from what we lack to what we have.

Slow Down. Embrace silence, turn off distractions, listen for God's still, small voice.

Rest in God's Love. Memorize Scriptures such as Psalm 23 and let them remind you that God provides.

Celebrate Others. Instead of comparing, cheer on the successes of others. Their victory doesn't diminish your value.

Stay Present. Don't live in the "someday." Find beauty in today's ordinary moments.

A Peaceful Conclusion

The ache for more doesn't have to win. Contentment is possible—not in ourselves, but in Christ. He is enough. He always has been and He always will be.

Tonight, as I prepare to rest, I breathe deeply. The striving subsides, the comparisons quiet. My prayer is simple: "God, teach me to live content. Remind me You are enough."

And for the first time in a long time, it feels true.

Psychological and Mental Health[1]

A lack of contentment is closely linked to feelings of loneliness, depression, and anxiety. Chronic loneliness, for instance, has been associated with increased risks of depression and suicidal thoughts. A study based on the English Longitudinal Study of Ageing found that nearly one in five individuals who reported being lonely had developed signs of depression within a year.

Moreover, individuals experiencing loneliness often report poor sleep quality, which can impair daily functioning. Loneliness has also been linked to schizoid personality disorder, where individuals may perceive the world differently and experience social alienation.

1 For more information see the following articles, accessed December 4, 2025, https://pmc.ncbi.nlm.nih.gov/articles/PMC9918825/; https://hsph.harvard.edu/news/spirituality-better-health-outcomes-patient-care/; https://thethrivecenter.org/how-are-mental-physical-and-spiritual-health-related/.

15 DREAMS DON'T COME TRUE

> *"But if we want to find joyful contentment, we're going to have to have some of those painful conversations with God, and to let go of the things that are taking his place in our lives."*
>
> **—Jennie Pollock**[20]

A text message in our family feed grabbed everyone's attention.

My day was packed. I had only thirty minutes before a dinner gathering, so I tapped the link on my phone. It was a two-hour compilation of videos from our three sons' younger years.

I watched the long-ago, long-haired me—coaching them in basketball and baseball.

And the they-are-so-cute them—young, so young, full of energy, laughter spilling over into every frame.

Birthday parties. Family conversations. Ordinary moments that, back then, didn't feel extraordinary at all.

I fast-forwarded through a few clips, then slowed down to watch a few more. The rest would have to wait.

---

20 Jennie Pollock, *If Only: Finding Joyful Contentment in the Face of Lack and Longing* (Epsom, Surrey, England: The Good Book Company, 2020), 67.

Those clips were old. Which meant we are now old.

I began thinking about the dreams we had for them, the dreams they had for themselves. Little boys dribbling basketballs on the court, imagining they'd one day play in packed arenas. Swinging bats, believing a major league home run was inevitable.

The practicing. The playing. The dreaming. And now—the remembering.

Not everyone sees their dreams come true. Not every MVP in a kids league makes the Big League. Not all big hopes become realities.

Maybe that's okay.

Because somewhere in those years, character was being formed. And sometimes that's the greater victory—that contentment can dwell even when dreams take different paths.

If new clips were made today, maybe we'd still smile just as deeply. Even if no impressive titles ever flashed on the screen, maybe we'd still smile.

The dreams in those old clips aren't so different from the dreams in all our lives.

We grow up with dreams, don't we?

Some are simple: a home, a steady job, a few friends who really see us. Some are ambitious: a platform, a ministry, a legacy, a creative work that changes the world. Some are deeply personal: marriage, children, healing, reconciliation.

But what happens when those dreams remain unattainable? What happens when the prayers go unanswered, the doors stay closed, the timeline stretches long?

We're left wondering whether contentment can live in that space.

The space where what we hoped for hasn't arrived?

The space where what we feared has?

Can contentment come during the tension of unmet expectations?

The Biblical Reality of Unfulfilled Longings

The Bible is full of people who lived with dreams that were delayed—or denied.

Moses dreamed of leading the people into the Promised Land. But he only saw it from a distance. David dreamed of building the temple. But that wasn't his assignment. Paul longed to be delivered from the thorn in his flesh. But the answer was grace, not removal.

And even Jesus, in the Garden, prayed:

> *"Father, if you are willing, take this cup from me; yet not my will, but yours be done."* (Luke 22:42)

Unfulfilled longings are not signs of failure. They are the soil where surrender grows.

Let's Ask Habakkuk

If you haven't read the book of Habakkuk in a while, pause here. Go read it—all three chapters.

Don't rush through it. Let the words move slowly across your mind and heart. Let yourself feel the ache, the confusion, the waiting, the hope. Read the cries, the questions, the complaints, the wonder. It's only three chapters, but it's an entire journey—a poetic, personal conversation with God.

Okay. Good. You read it.

Now, how does that fit here in this book? What does that ancient conversation have to do with contentment? How can an honest dialogue with the all-knowing, all-powerful, always present, always aware God carry us from disappointment toward gratitude—even when, or especially when, our dreams don't come true?

Habakkuk lived in days of darkness—when leaders were corrupt, justice was twisted, and hope felt far away.

He didn't preach to the people; he talked to God. He didn't shout in the streets; he cried in prayer.

"Why do You let this happen?" he asked. "How long must I wait for You to make things right?"

His words were poems of lament—honest, aching, desperate.

And God listened.

The first response came like thunder: "I am doing something you wouldn't believe even if I told you." God would use Babylon—yes, that Babylon—to bring judgment on Judah.

That answer didn't fit neatly in a sermon.

So Habakkuk asked again: "How can You use a nation even more wicked than we are?" Then he climbed the watchtower to wait for God's reply.

And God did reply.

"Write it down," He said. "There is a time appointed. Though it lingers, wait for it. It will certainly come."

The vision was this: Babylon, and every nation like Babylon, will fall beneath the weight of its own violence and pride. But the righteous will live by faith.

Habakkuk lived in a season of injustice, confusion, and fear. He saw what was wrong with the world and what was broken within himself. He wanted answers. He wanted God to fix what was wrong. He wanted a clear path and a fast solution.

But instead he received an invitation. Not to understand everything. But to trust the One who does.

God didn't silence Habakkuk's questions, those prayers of lament—He met them. God didn't erase the pain—He entered it. God didn't stop the waiting—He stayed in it with Habakkuk.

And somewhere in that ongoing, unfinished conversation, Habakkuk began to trust. His circumstances didn't improve, but his vision did. He began to see that even when nothing made sense, God was still writing the story. He began to discover a deeper kind of peace—not the peace that comes when everything works out, but the peace that comes when we remember who holds it all together.

Maybe this is where we begin learning contentment. Not in our successes or in our dreams fulfilled, but in our honest, ongoing dialogue with God.

We talk. We listen. We wait. We keep coming back.

Ask.

Trust.

Wait.

What can we learn from that story? What should we do?

Bring our honest questions to God. Trust God's bigger plan. Wait with expectation.

These aren't just spiritual disciplines; they're survival rhythms. They teach us to breathe again, to slow down, to hand over our illusions of control and hold tightly to the faith that God is still here.

When the dreams don't come true, faith doesn't demand that we pretend we're okay. Faith invites us to bring our questions, our confusion, and our pain to the One who sees the whole picture. Faith is daring to bring our ache to God. Faith is believing God is at work even when His timeline and strategy don't match ours.

And we begin to sense what Habakkuk found—that even if the fig tree does not bud, even if the fields are empty and the barns are bare, there is still joy to be found, not in what we've lost, but in the One who never leaves.

That's the quiet gift of contentment: not the removal of longing, but the restoration of trust. Not the absence of pain, but the presence of peace. Not everything we wanted, but everything we need.

The book ends not with anger but with a song. Even if the fields are empty, even if the vineyards produce nothing, "I will rejoice in the Lord."

Habakkuk began by crying, "How long?"

He ended by singing, "I will wait."

A poetic conversation turned into a song of trust.

Maybe that's the invitation for us, too. To bring our questions. To trust His timing. To wait for it.

God's promises may seem slow, but they never fail.

A Personal Story

There were dreams I believed were from God—ones I still believe were good.

Dreams of impact. Dreams of healing. Dreams of more. And yet ... some didn't happen. Some still haven't. Some probably never will.

I remember sitting in a quiet chapel, wrestling with disappointment, asking why.

Why not now?

Why not ever?

And in the stillness came not an answer, but an invitation.

An invitation to trust.

To trust that what has happened is enough. To trust that what God is doing is still good. To trust that what remains unseen is not wasted.

And you? What about your dreams? You heard a speaker who inspired you, a friend who encouraged you, a leader who motivated you, an inner confidence that stirred you, an external confirmation that verified you.

But now? You continue your residence in the city of *not yet*. Or maybe in the community of *never*. You have prayed and worked. You have invested and persisted. You have refused to quit and chosen to remain.

But the *not yet* or the *never* stare back at you.

I can assure you of this: Your personal story isn't over. I can also declare this: It might not end the way you wish.

How will you respond?

The Practice: Contentment in the Middle

Sometimes we think we can only be content when:

- We get the job.
- We get the spouse.
- We get the breakthrough.
- We get the recognition.

But real contentment is what happens in the middle. When the dreams are foggy. When the outcome is unclear. When the wait is long.

How do we live it out?

- Name the dream.
- Write it down. Say it out loud. Be honest with God about the longing.
- Grieve what hasn't been.
- Contentment isn't denial. It's honesty with hope. Let yourself feel the sadness—then release it to the One who holds all time.
- Celebrate what is.
- Look around. What's already good? What's already here? What deserves a thank you?
- Return to the present.
- Unmet dreams often pull us into the future or trap us in the past. Contentment brings us home to today.

> *"Not that I speak in regard to need, for I have learned in whatever state I am, to be content."* (Philippians 4:11, NKJV)

Paul wrote that while imprisoned. While limited. While dreams of ministry expansion were on hold. Yet he had learned the secret: Christ is enough.

Still Dreaming, Still Trusting

What do we do when the dream doesn't arrive? When the door doesn't open? When the prayer seems unanswered and the ending isn't what we wrote in our minds?

We breathe. We grieve. We loosen our grip. We name the loss and let Jesus sit with us in it. And then slowly, sometimes very slowly, we begin to see again.

Maybe the dream was good, but not the best. Maybe the delay is shaping a situation, or us, for something deeper. Maybe the detour itself births a dream we never knew we needed.

This isn't about giving up. This is about looking up. Not pretending the pain isn't real, but trusting God still is. Not forcing a silver lining, but finding His steady presence in the gray. Not needing to understand everything, but learning to receive what is.

Because when dreams don't come true, the God who gave you the ability to dream is still with you. And, sometimes, contentment is born in that very place where surrender meets grace, where hope begins again, where life is seen through a new lens, where who you were is transforming into the new person you're becoming, where what seemed to matter most just isn't as important anymore.

The dreams may not have come true. But maybe something truer is coming alive in you. And maybe that's a better dream after all.

Contentment is not the absence of longing. It's the presence of peace and assurance and trust—even in the longing—no matter the outcome.

This isn't a call to let go of every dream. It's a call to hold them differently.

To place them in open hands. To let God shape their fulfillment—or their transformation. To trust that He writes better stories than we ever imagined.

Practical Steps to Head off Discontentment

1. Acknowledge and Reflect.

- Step: Take time to identify areas of discontentment in your life. Write down what you feel dissatisfied with and why.
- Benefit: Awareness is the first step to change. Reflection helps pinpoint specific causes rather than vague feelings.

2. Turn to Gratitude.

- Step: List three things you're thankful for every day, no matter how small they seem.
- Benefit: Gratitude shifts your focus from what's missing to what's present, fostering a mindset of abundance and joy.

3. Shift Perspective.

- Step: Ask yourself, "What does this teach me about God's provision or purpose?" Focus on trusting His timing and plan.
- Benefit: A faith-based perspective reminds you that your identity and worth are found in God, not circumstances or possessions.

4. Limit Comparisons.

- Step: Take a break from social media or anything that fuels envy and comparison.
- Benefit: Eliminating triggers helps you focus on your unique journey rather than measuring yourself against others.

5. Simplify and Declutter.

- Step: Organize your home, schedule, and commitments to eliminate unnecessary distractions or burdens.
- Benefit: Simplifying life can bring clarity and appreciation for what truly matters.

6. Adjust Expectations.

- Step: Ask if your goals or desires are realistic or necessary. Reframe your expectations to focus on sufficiency rather than excess.
- Benefit: Helps reduce pressure and disappointment, making space for peace and contentment.

7. Cultivate Spiritual Practices.

- Step: Spend time daily in prayer, Bible reading, or meditating on Scriptures such as Philippians 4:11–13 or Psalm 23.
- Benefit: Reconnecting with God's promises reminds you of His sufficiency and helps calm discontentment.

8. Focus on Serving Others.

- Step: Volunteer, encourage a friend, or meet someone else's need.
- Benefit: Serving others shifts the focus away from self and fosters joy in making a difference.

9. Set Healthy Boundaries.

- Step: Protect your time and energy by saying "no" to unnecessary commitments or unhealthy influences.
- Benefit: Reduces stress and allows you to focus on what brings true fulfillment.

10. Celebrate Progress.

- Step: Recognize and appreciate small victories or changes in attitude as you work toward contentment.
- Benefit: Reinforces positive behavior and keeps you motivated.

11. Seek Community Support.

- Step: Talk to trusted friends, mentors, or a pastor about your feelings and seek their encouragement.
- Benefit: Accountability and shared wisdom provide perspective and strength in your journey.

12. Develop Patience and Trust.

- Step: Embrace seasons of waiting or lack as opportunities to grow in faith and trust God's provision.
- Benefit: Builds resilience and a deeper relationship with God, as contentment often grows in challenging seasons.

13. Embrace Contentment as a Discipline.

- Step: Intentionally practice finding satisfaction in the present even when it feels unnatural. Say aloud, "I have enough, and God is enough."
- Benefit: Over time, this mindset becomes second nature, leading to greater peace and joy.

By taking these intentional steps, you can move toward a life marked by contentment, joy, and trust in God's provision.

16
GRATITUDE

"We can't be naive about the wilderness; it's a dangerous place. But we must never avoid the wilderness; it's a wonderful place."
—Eugene H. Peterson[21]

Gratitude transforms everything.

It's the heartbeat of contentment. Without it, we'll find ourselves grumbling, comparing, longing for what we don't have, while overlooking the gifts right in front of us.

We've all had moments when we saw something ordinary with fresh eyes—a child's laughter, a friend's call, the warmth of the sun, the beauty of a familiar view. And in those moments we realized how rich we already are.

The key to deep contentment is gratitude.

Not the surface-level "thank you" we offer when we get something we want. But a deeper, more abiding sense of thankfulness that fills our hearts with peace regardless of our circumstances.

---

21 Eugene H. Peterson, *Leap Over the Wall: Earthy Spirituality for Everyday Christians* (San Francisco, CA: HarperSanFrancisco, 1997), 80.

The Bible and Gratitude

Scripture is rich with calls to gratitude. God didn't just suggest it as a nice idea. He commanded it because He knew what it would do for us.

I have included this verse before, but it fits here again:

> *"Give thanks in all circumstances; for this is God's will for you in Christ Jesus"* (1 Thessalonians 5:18).

This verse isn't conditional. It doesn't say, "Give thanks when things are good." It says, "Give thanks in all circumstances."

That means even when dreams are delayed, when disappointment lingers, when we can't make sense of what's happening around us, gratitude is still possible. And it is the pathway to contentment.

Practicing Gratitude

Gratitude isn't a passive feeling that happens to come over us. It's an active choice. The more we choose it, the more it becomes a natural response, a way of seeing the world.

Here's how we can cultivate it:

- Start each day with gratitude.
- Wake up and list three things you're thankful for. It could be simple—your morning coffee—or significant—such as health or family. Try writing them down in a journal. Naming our blessings helps us see them more clearly.
- Be present to the small things.
- Gratitude grows when we pay attention. Notice the smile of a stranger. Hear the laughter of children. Feel the warmth of a hug. These are the moments that make life full.
- Gratitude in trials.
- This is the hardest part. But it's also the most transformative. In times of difficulty gratitude doesn't deny the pain, but it shifts our focus from what's wrong to what's still good.
- Express gratitude to others.

- Gratitude isn't meant to stay within. Tell someone you appreciate them. Send a note. Call a friend. A simple "thank you" can change the course of a conversation and bring joy to both the giver and receiver.

A Challenge: Gratitude in the Ordinary

The days go by quickly, don't they? Sometimes it's easy to miss the beauty in the routine. But every moment holds something worth thanking God for. The challenge is not to wait for extraordinary moments to express gratitude but to be thankful in the ordinary.

Gratitude turns ordinary into extraordinary. It turns mundane into meaningful.

When we open our hearts to gratitude, we are planting seeds for lasting contentment.

When Words Weigh Us Down

Some voices lift us.

Some voices drain us.

And sometimes the heaviest voice is our own.

In a world flooded with negativity, it's easy to join the noise without even noticing. But maybe it's time to pause. To listen. To rethink the words we speak and the weight they carry.

We've all heard them. We've all known them. We've all been them.

Those voices.

As I've written and said many times, but as I should apply better than I do: The voices we hear influence the choices we make.

So many voices.

Negative about the news. Negative about the weather. Negative about the church. About the umpires, the prices, the leaders. The everything.

We carry conversations like baggage.

And many of those conversations—whether spoken or thought—drag us down. Heavy. Critical. Draining. We speak them. We listen to them. We replay them. And slowly, subtly, they shape us.

Negativity becomes normal. We convince ourselves it's honesty. We justify it as insight. But it's often neither.

It's just noise.

Noise that steals joy. Noise that drowns peace. Noise that keeps us from hearing truth.

Spiritually? It clogs our ability to hear from God.

Mentally? It becomes a loop of complaint and comparison.

Physically? It stiffens our posture and exhausts our bones.

Relationally? It shuts down connection before it begins.

This must change!

> *"Do not let any unwholesome talk come out of your mouths," Paul wrote, "but only what is helpful for building others up according to their needs, that it may benefit those who listen."* (Ephesians 4:29)

Not everything needs to be said. Not every opinion helps. Not every complaint leads to change. But every word carries weight.

Let's begin here and now:

- **Notice it:** Catch the moment your tone shifts. Catch the sigh. The sarcasm. The subtle jab.
- **Name it:** Not with shame, but with honesty. That didn't help. That didn't heal. That didn't build up.
- **Replace it:** Speak truth wrapped in kindness. Speak gratitude when complaint feels easier. Speak hope when the world says despair.

Not because everything is perfect.

But because grace is present even in the mess.

Let's become people who lighten the weight, not add to it. Let's offer words that lift. That bless. That breathe life. Because the people around us—ourselves included—are already carrying enough.

Let's speak less like critics and more like builders. Let's notice what we're saying—and what we're becoming because of it.

This world is already heavy.

Let's not add to the weight. Let's choose gratitude. Let's speak life.

Fifty Thoughts on Contentment

1. Contentment isn't about finding the perfect life; it's about learning to live well in the imperfect one you already have.
2. Restless souls seek applause from crowds, but contentment is found in the quiet approval of the Father.
3. Jesus didn't run faster to win a race. He walked slower to heal the broken—shouldn't we do the same?
4. The noise of success drowns out the whisper of peace; contentment listens for the whisper.
5. Like the early church waiting for the Wind, contentment comes when we stop striving and start trusting.
6. When dissatisfaction tells you to keep chasing, contentment invites you to sit down and breathe.
7. True contentment is letting go of what you can't control and holding tightly to the God who controls it all.
8. The applause of people is fleeting, but the love of Jesus echoes into eternity.
9. When you leave the crowd like Jesus did, you find the quiet place where contentment waits.
10. Goals are good guides but terrible masters—don't let them steal today's joy.

11. Contentment isn't the absence of ambition; it's the presence of peace no matter the outcome.
12. The danger of dissatisfaction is that it blinds us to the gifts we already hold.
13. Stop chasing success long enough to notice the small wins that are already around you.
14. When life feels overwhelming, contentment is the courage to say, "This is enough for now."
15. The love of Jesus is enough, but we only feel it when we stop looking for more.
16. Like the disciples waiting in the upper room, contentment requires patience for the Wind to move.
17. The moment you stop comparing your life to others is the moment contentment can breathe again.
18. Real joy isn't found in reaching the next milestone but in savoring the step you're on.
19. When the world demands more of you, contentment gently reminds you that you already belong.
20. The rhythm of contentment beats slower than success, but leads to a healthier heart.
21. In the selfish pursuit of more, we lose sight of the sacred ***enough***.
22. Jesus didn't need the crowd's approval to feel loved; neither do you.
23. When expectations weigh heavy, contentment lightens the load by pointing to grace.
24. Like rain refreshing dry ground, contentment renews the soul in seasons of waiting.

25. You don't have to prove your worth to anyone; contentment comes when you realize you're already loved.
26. The hurried life leaves no room for gratitude; contentment grows in the soil of thanksgiving.
27. Dissatisfaction whispers, "You're not enough;" contentment shouts, "You're more than enough in Christ."
28. Contentment isn't laziness; it's choosing to work hard while trusting God with the results.
29. Even in the mess, contentment sees the masterpiece God is creating in you.
30. The Wind of God doesn't blow through frantic schedules; it finds the still hearts waiting.
31. Success without contentment is a hollow victory; peace without success is a deeper joy.
32. Contentment doesn't deny the struggle; it learns to rest in God through the struggle.
33. Every moment—no matter how ordinary—is a chance to choose joy and call it holy.
34. The crowd will always want more from you, but contentment reminds you to rest with the Father.
35. Let today's blessings be enough; tomorrow's worries can wait.
36. Contentment doesn't eliminate goals; it reframes them with gratitude and grace.
37. Joy isn't found in what's next; it's found in what's now.
38. The early church waited for the Wind; can we learn to wait for God's timing, too?
39. Dissatisfaction is a thief robbing us of peace—don't let it win.

40. The secret to contentment is this: you don't need to be more because Jesus already is.
41. Even when life feels small, contentment sees it as sacred.
42. Walk away from the chaos, find your quiet, and let contentment meet you there.
43. Contentment isn't complacency; it's confidence in God's goodness right where you are.
44. The applause of heaven is far sweeter than the fleeting cheers of earth.
45. Life is messy, but contentment learns to love the mess as part of the masterpiece.
46. When you feel overwhelmed, ask yourself: What would Jesus do? He would pause.
47. The book of Acts teaches us to wait; contentment teaches us to trust while we do.
48. You won't find contentment in the chase; you'll find it in the stillness.
49. Success may feel satisfying for a moment, but only contentment offers lasting joy.
50. Jesus' love is enough. It always was. It always will be. Let that truth quiet your soul.

17

SERVING OTHERS

"When a Christian's heartstrings are wound on this heavenly frame of contentment, then it is fit for duty." —**Thomas Watson**[22]

The elderly lady regularly asks what she can do to help someone else. The young man often asks what he can do to assist those living in a retirement center. The married couple takes others to lunch every Sunday after church. The student goes out of her way to help other students feel welcome. The retired minister has found other ways to minister off stage, unknown, no pulpit in sight.

I could write a list and it would be long. We could include pictures and stories. They would fill the pages. We could offer dates and times. You would want to attend.

But we'd be missing the point. We'd miss the true reason their names and tasks are included on the list.

They do not want others to know what they are doing. They don't want to be known. They just want to serve.

What would that catalogue include? Acts of service to others. Those times when people serve others, expecting nothing in return. Those

22 Thomas Watson, *The Art of Divine Contentment: In Modern English*, translation and annotations by Jason Roth (Oswego, IL: Godlipress, 2017), 77.

moments when people do unto others what no one might ever do unto them. Those moments when people give like Jesus, live like Jesus, sacrifice like Jesus, serve like Jesus.

I've seen their faces. I've heard their voices. I've smelled their sweat. I've known their giving. I've received their care.

They listen. They provide. They visit. They wait. They don't preach a sermon. They serve in action.

Crowds might not hear their songs, but they keep singing to a few who need their music. Benevolent people might not fill their financial investments or savings accounts, but they invest time and interest in the lives of those who need friends and food. Former students might not contact her to show appreciation for her extra time after school, her willingness to listen, and her sincere concern for their development, but she thinks about her decades in the classrooms and lives without regret.

Serving. That's the way. That's the lifestyle. That's the what and the why.

Contentment is not just an internal state. It's meant to overflow into the world around us.

It's easy to think that contentment is just about getting our own needs met—achieving personal happiness or comfort. But true contentment is found in giving, in serving, in loving others without expecting anything in return.

Serving others shifts the focus from self to others and, in that shift, we find a deeper sense of fulfillment.

In fact, contentment isn't complete until it's shared.

Contentment doesn't exist in isolation. It thrives in community, in connection, in lifting others up.

The Biblical Call to Service

Jesus modeled this for us. He didn't come to be served, but to serve. He didn't live for His own gain, but for the good of others.

> *"For even the Son of Man did not come to be served, but to serve, and to give his life as a ransom for many"* (Mark 10:45).

Jesus understood that the way to true life—the way to contentment—is not through selfish pursuit but through selfless giving. And this kind of giving—whether through acts of kindness, love, time, or resources—leads to the greatest fulfillment.

Practicing Service

We can't serve everyone, but we can serve someone. When we choose to focus on others, we find that contentment comes, not through receiving, but through giving. The more we serve, the more we are served by the joy that comes from helping others.

Here's how we can live this out:

1. **Serve in small ways.**

   Sometimes we think service needs to be grand or dramatic. But often it's the little acts that make the biggest difference. Hold the door open. Offer a smile. Send a kind message. Give a thoughtful gift. These small actions create big waves of change.

2. **Volunteer your time.**

   Whether it's a local food bank, a children's home, or a neighbor who needs help, volunteer your time. The more we step outside ourselves, the more we find purpose and contentment.

3. **Listen more than you speak.**

   Sometimes serving others means simply being present. Listen to their stories. Hear their struggles. Let them know they're seen and loved. Sometimes, just showing up is enough.

4. **Serve without expecting anything in return.**

   The greatest form of service is the one given freely, without strings attached. It's the kind of service that doesn't ask for a thank-you or a reward but gives simply because we love.

At Once

This is a conversation about contentment from the other side of a miracle.[23]

I didn't go to Joppa. Joppa came to me.

Not through geography, not through time travel, but in a quiet moment on an ordinary morning—one of those days when restlessness tries to whisper that what I do is not enough. That what I offer is too small.

So I paused. I sat in my chair with a journal open and my Bible nearby. And I listened.

I imagined the voices from Acts 9. Not to create fiction, but to welcome their wisdom into my present.

Tabitha was first. She didn't talk like a saint or speak in scrolls. She spoke like someone who'd lived in kitchens and workshops, someone who knew the feel of thread and the ache of tired feet.

"I didn't chase miracles," she said. "I just kept doing what needed to be done."

I asked her if that made her feel content. She smiled. "Doing good was enough for me. I wasn't trying to impress anyone. I was just trying to help someone."

I thought of how many times I've measured my days by accomplishments. And here she was, reminding me that the content soul is the one who keeps serving when no one's looking. The one who sews grace into the edges of ordinary life.

Peter spoke next. Calm, honest, transformed.

"I didn't walk into that house knowing what would happen," he said. "But I did walk in trusting that prayer was more important than panic."

I asked him what kept him grounded. He said, "I remembered Jesus. That was enough."

23 See Acts 9:36–41.

It made me think that contentment isn't found in knowing the outcome, but in knowing the One who holds the outcome. Sometimes resurrection comes at once. Other times, the waiting is long. But peace doesn't have to wait.

Then the widows. Dozens of voices, layered in grief and gratitude.

"She made us feel seen," one said. "She didn't talk about generosity. She lived it," another added.

Their stories weren't about how Tabitha died. They were about how she lived. And there, again, I found contentment—not in the miracle, but in the meaning. Not in the spotlight, but in the stitching.

Finally, I asked them all: What would you say to those of us living in this noisy, rushed world, always striving, always reaching?

Tabitha spoke for them: "Be content to serve. Be content to love. Be content to trust that the little things matter."

Peter added, "Kneel often. Speak less. Believe more."

And the widows? "What she gave us was enough. And we carry it still."

The conversation faded. But its message didn't.

I sat in my quiet room surrounded by threads of their witness. And I realized that contentment is not found in the miracle we wait for. It's found in the life we live until the miracle. In the service done in secret. In the whispered prayer beside the bed. In the moment when we choose to say yes. Not later. Not someday.

At once.

The Joy of Serving

Serving others leads us into joy—not only because we're helping others, but because we are living out God's purpose for us. We are wired to love and care for others, and when we do so we find that our own hearts are full.

The more we give, the more we are blessed.

The more we serve, the more we become like Jesus.

Contentment is found not in being served but in serving. And when we live lives of service, we discover that the world is not only richer because of us, but we are richer because of it.

The Blessing That Gives Away

We often pray to be blessed.

But what if that prayer is incomplete?

What if true contentment comes not just from what we receive, but from what we release? Not from what we keep, but from what we give away?

It was a simple prayer at first: "Bless me, Lord."

I had whispered it in late nights and early mornings, in quiet moments and crowded rooms. It was honest. It was familiar. And it was mine. I prayed it when I didn't know what else to say. I prayed it when I was hungry—not for food, but for something more.

Peace. Stability. Provision. Security. Direction. I thought I was praying for contentment.

But the longer I sat with that prayer, the more I sensed it shifting.

Not because I didn't need the blessing. I did. But because I was starting to realize why I needed it.

One afternoon I sat with Psalm 67 open in front of me. And these words came alive, like they had been waiting for me to slow down enough to notice:

> *May God be gracious to us and bless us*
>
> *and make his face shine on us.*
>
> *So that Your ways may be known on earth,*
>
> *Your salvation among all nations* (Psalm 67:1–2).

There it was. A truth I hadn't fully seen before: The blessing I prayed for wasn't meant to stop with me. It was meant to flow through me.

God's goodness wasn't a personal possession; it was a global invitation. And suddenly, contentment took on a new shape.

I remembered a time years ago on a dusty road outside the city—a mission trip that had felt ordinary at the time. We handed out water bottles, played games with children, listened to stories through translators, and heard prayers prayed in languages we didn't understand. But there was this one older woman I'll never forget.

She had nothing by the world's standards.

No electricity. No shoes. No retirement plan.

But she glowed with joy.

She sang while she worked. She gave when she had so little. She welcomed us like we were family, not strangers from a far-off land.

As we left her small home, she grabbed my hand and said something.

The translator told me later: "Tell them God is good, and His face shines on us here, too."

She was blessed. But not with wealth. Not with comfort.

She was blessed with something deeper—the contentment of knowing she was seen by God, and the desire that others might know Him too. She had Psalm 67 written in her life story.

That is the secret we often miss.

We keep searching for contentment in what we can gain. God invites us to find it in what we can give.

To be content not because we have all we want—but because we are part of something bigger. To rejoice not only in the gift—but in the Giver's mission. To receive the blessing—so that all people may know Him, praise Him, and find joy in Him.

May the peoples praise you, God;
may all the peoples praise you. (v. 3)

That's the prayer now.

I still ask Him to bless me. But I ask Him to bless me for the sake of others. To bless me not just with more, but with a heart open wide enough to give more away.

That's where contentment lives. Not in what we hold, but in what we release. Not in keeping the light, but in letting it shine on others. Not in praying smaller prayers, but in stepping into God's wider vision.

And maybe what I was searching for all along—peace, purpose, satisfaction, joy—was never missing.

It was already mine.

It was already His.

I just had to share it.

Because the deepest contentment often begins when we stop asking, "What can I get?" and start asking, "How can I serve?"

Practical Examples of Contentment

1. **Accepting Your Circumstances:** A single person who desires marriage, but embraces their season of singleness by focusing on personal growth, serving others, and trusting God's timing.
2. **Finding Joy in the Little Things:** Enjoying a simple meal with loved ones and being grateful for the moment, rather than wishing for a fancier lifestyle or gourmet food.
3. **Living Within Your Means:** A family choosing a modest vacation that fits their budget—instead of going into debt for a luxury trip—and enjoying the time together fully.

4. **Being Grateful for Your Job:** A person working a less glamorous job, but taking pride in his or her work, seeing it as an opportunity to provide for their family and grow in character.

5. **Rejoicing in Others' Success:** Celebrating a friend's promotion or new house without feeling envious, trusting that your own blessings will come in due time.

6. **Staying Present:** A mother cherishing time with her children at home rather than longing for the "freedom" of life before parenthood.

7. **Choosing Patience in Trials:** A person battling illness or facing financial hardship choosing to trust God and focus on what they still have, rather than dwelling on what they've lost.

8. **Practicing Gratitude over Complaints:** Thanking God for a reliable car even if it's old, rather than complaining about not having a new one.

9. **Refusing to Compare:** A student celebrating their own academic progress instead of comparing themselves to peers with higher grades or achievements.

10. **Finding Fulfillment in Serving:** A retiree spending time volunteering in their community, content with their life stage instead of wishing for the career days of the past.

18

LIVING WITH LESS

"Contentment reminds you to fix your thoughts on what really matters and move toward those things." **—Rachel Cruze**[24]

Facial expression. Tone of voice. Body language.

We've all seen it.

We've all done it.

That person walks into the room and suddenly our hidden competition isn't quite so hidden. Jealousy has a way of slipping out—in avoidance, in subtle distance, in a too-harsh tone, in the quiet roll of the eyes, in words that sound like jokes but sting like envy, in gossip masked as concern, in bitterness disguised as self-protection.

We could add more methods, but the point is this: Rather than welcoming that old response, what if we simply waved goodbye to a life of comparison?

Higher scores win in ball games. But in life? Less is often more. Especially when less is chosen. Especially when contentment doesn't come from labels or rankings or numbers. Especially when spiritual depth matters more than financial or social status.

24 Rachel Cruze, *The Contentment Journal* (Mahwah, NJ: Ramsey Press, 2019).

Why do we keep reaching for more? Why can't enough be enough? And how can we train our hearts to find joy in what already is?

This chapter explores the beauty of living with less—not as punishment, but as invitation. Not scarcity, but simplicity. Not loss, but freedom.

More doesn't always mean better.

In a culture built on accumulation, we're taught to believe that contentment comes from more. More money. More followers. More possessions. More likes. More influence.

But more can be a mirage.

We often don't need more.

We need less.

Less noise. Less clutter. Less comparison. Less distraction.

The truth is that living with less often leads to living with more peace.

Jesus and Simplicity

Jesus didn't live a life of excess. He walked dusty roads, spoke with strangers, and traveled light. He taught people to stop storing up treasures on earth and instead to seek the kingdom of God first.

> *"Do not store up for yourselves treasures on earth ... But store up for yourselves treasures in heaven ... For where your treasure is, there your heart will be also."* (Matthew 6:19–21)

Jesus wasn't against possessions—He was against misplaced priorities. He knew how easily our hearts are drawn toward the temporary. He knew the weight of too much stuff, too much striving, too much chasing.

The Practice of Less

Living with less is a practice in resistance. We resist the cultural pull toward more and choose something richer.

Here are a few ways to practice "less" in your daily life:

- Declutter your space.
- Clean out a drawer, a closet, a room. Get rid of what you don't need. Create space that invites peace.
- Pause before purchasing.
- Ask yourself, *Do I really need this? Will it bring lasting joy or just temporary satisfaction?* Let that question guide your decisions.
- Unplug intentionally.
- Limit screen time. Turn off notifications. Be present to the moment you're in.
- Spend intentionally.
- Invest in experiences, not just things. Choose generosity over accumulation. Use your resources to bless others.
- Value Sabbath and stillness.
- Rest. Don't fill every hour. Create time where you do nothing "productive" and learn to be okay with it.

The Surprise of Less

Here's the surprise: When we choose less, we discover more.

More space.

More peace.

More clarity.

More time for what matters.

More attention to people and purpose right in front of us.

Living with less doesn't mean missing out. It means focusing in.

Ending a chapter with fewer words doesn't always prove that less is more ... but in this case, maybe it does.

If you begin—even slowly, even inconsistently—to live with less in the right way and for the right reasons, you may find you're holding more than ever before.

More peace. More time. More presence. More trust. More joy. More Jesus.

So try it. End the chapter. Apply the ideas. Begin living with less—less noise, less comparison, less pressure to prove. Make space where stuff once filled. Choose simplicity not as punishment, but as a path to peace.

Wave goodbye to the performance, the pressure, the pursuit—and there, in the silence that follows, contentment nods its head and stays.

I thought about that wave the day I packed up my office to move into a different office. Letting go wasn't just an idea. It was a reality. It was box after box of books—volumes I'd read, quoted, taught from, carried through seasons of my life. My hands knew their weight. My shelves had memorized their spines.

But my new office was smaller. No matter how I stacked or rearranged, there wasn't enough space. Something had to go.

I sat on the floor, surrounded by boxes. I ran my hand along book covers, remembering when I'd bought them, taught them, lived them. Some I kept. Some I gave away. The box flaps closed with a hollow thud—the sound of goodbye.

Living with less often feels like loss at first. But as I carried fewer boxes into my new office, my chest felt lighter. My steps steadier. And something shifted: What I gave away didn't diminish me; it made space for something new.

Maybe that's part of contentment. To hand things down—to bless someone else—we often must release what we've been gripping. Books, clothes, dreams, roles. Titles, agendas, schedules, vision. Collections, preferences, objectives, delights.

Even versions of ourselves we once thought we had to be.

Contentment through the Year[1]

January: The year begins with a fresh calendar and clean pages, yet the chill of winter whispers reminders of waiting. January teaches us that contentment isn't found in doing more but in being present. As we celebrate Epiphany, let us find joy in the small, quiet ways Christ reveals Himself—like the Magi, who followed a star and knelt in worship.

February: With Valentine's Day, love often takes center stage, but February invites us to seek a deeper love—the unconditional love of Christ. In the cold or lingering gray, contentment grows in the warmth of gratitude for the relationships we have—and in remembering we are never alone.

March: As spring tiptoes in, March reminds us that new life comes in slow, steady steps. Lent calls us to pause, reflect, and let go of the unnecessary. Contentment blooms when we embrace simplicity and wait for resurrection moments, even when the ground still looks barren.

April: Easter bursts forth, proclaiming victory and hope. Contentment flourishes here, where the empty tomb declares that death does not win and our striving can cease. The world awakens with vibrant colors, and we are invited to live with joy, rooted in the power of the resurrection.

May: May's warmth brings graduations, celebrations, and Mother's Day—a time to honor growth, gratitude, and sacrifice. The blooming flowers whisper that contentment is cultivated in seasons of nurture, trust, and faithful care.

June: Summer arrives, with long days and time for connection. June invites us to rest in the ordinary—barbecues, walks, and laughter shared under the sun. Father's Day encourages us to remember the steady love of our Heavenly Father, a love that quiets our restless hearts.

1 Note: Many holidays celebrated throughout the year in the United States are celebrated in other countries, but may have different names and dates.

July: Independence Day reminds us of freedom, but contentment calls us to live free from comparison and worry. In the heat of July, rest feels sweeter and gratitude for simple joys—like shade and water—grounds us in the moment.

August: As summer lingers, August often feels like a transitional month. Contentment in August means embracing the now while preparing for what's next. The rhythm of life isn't about rushing but finding beauty in the in-between moments.

September: Autumn begins to whisper, and with it comes the reminder that change is inevitable. Contentment learns to let go, to find peace in seasons of transition. The simplicity of Labor Day rest reminds us that our value is not tied to our work but to who we are in Christ.

October: Crisp air and falling leaves remind us that beauty comes in letting go. Contentment in October invites us to celebrate the harvest—the tangible and spiritual fruits of God's faithfulness—and rest in the assurance that He provides.

November: Gratitude takes center stage in November, with Thanksgiving inviting us to reflect on our blessings. Contentment grows when we choose to give thanks, not for perfect circumstances but for God's presence in every circumstance.

December: Advent and Christmas declare the arrival of Emmanuel—God with us. Contentment in December means slowing down amid the chaos, marveling at the mystery of the incarnation, and receiving the gift of Jesus with open, grateful hearts.

19

BUILDING HABITS OF CONTENTMENT

"It is the duty of all Christians to strive after contentment every single day for the rest of their lives on earth." **—Andrew W. Davis**[25]

The server did not ask for my order. She saw my face, smiled, and wrote down my order. Then she turned to the others sitting with me at the table and asked what they wanted.

She knew me. She knew what I would order. She knew what I would not order. And she was correct.

If you know me, you know this: I am predictable. I budget my schedules, allowing a certain amount of time daily or weekly for my five jobs. I adjust my routines, hoping for a healthy equilibrium.

But life in ministry—like any life, really—is bombarded with surprises. We learn to adapt, to adjust, to reschedule. A financial crisis walks right in the front door without knocking. A health issue reaches over to grab us with no advance notice. A traffic jam makes us late. A cancelled flight makes us very late. A friend in crisis becomes the place our attention must go. A baby is born. A loved one passes away. A boss calls you into the office.

25 Andrew W. Davis, *The Power of Christian Contentment: Finding Deeper, Richer, Christ-Centered Joy* (Grand Rapids, MI: Baker Books, 2019), 40.

You know those times, those surprises, those seasons.

But you probably also know this: we are much better at adapting and adjusting to change when we have structure—wise time management, healthy habits, sound budgets, and hearts of contentment. Building habits of contentment can positively alter our life direction.

And those habits don't just appear out of nowhere.

Contentment doesn't happen by accident.

We don't drift into contentment. We grow into it.

One decision at a time. One day at a time. One practice at a time.

Habits shape us—even the small ones. And when we build our lives around consistent rhythms of peace, gratitude, and intentional living, contentment stops being a distant ideal and becomes a lived reality.

What Are You Rehearsing?

Every habit is a kind of rehearsal. When we rehearse anxiety, we become anxious. When we rehearse hurry, we become exhausted. But when we rehearse contentment, we become whole.

Let's hear Paul the apostle again. He said it like this: "I have learned the secret of being content in any and every situation" (Philippians 4:12).

Did you notice the word, "learned"?

Contentment is a *learned* habit. A practiced way of being.

Small Habits with Lasting Impact

Here are a few practical habits that help contentment take root:

1. **Morning Stillness:** Begin your day *without* your phone.

   Read a verse. Sit in silence. Write a prayer. Let your soul breathe before the world demands your attention.

2. **Gratitude Notes:** Each day, write down three things you're thankful for. Don't overthink it. Gratitude grows stronger when named often.

3. **The "Enough" Reminder:** Place a sticky note on your bathroom mirror, your dashboard, or your computer that simply says, "You don't need more to be enough."

   Let that truth interrupt your craving for more.

4. **Digital Fasts:** Pick one day a week to be mostly offline. Or start with one evening. Let your mind rest from constant input.

5. **Generosity Moments:** Each week look for one small way to give—your time, your attention, your resources. Generosity loosens the grip of self and invites contentment in.

6. **Sabbath Joy:** Set aside a block of time to rest. No production. No pressure. Just joy. Learn to delight in the gifts God has already given.

The Hidden Cost of Holding On: A Story About Honesty, Habits, and Healing

He knew it was time to cut the cord.

Not just with a toxic subscription or a habit that had quietly become harmful. But deeper than that. Emotional attachments had latched onto his heart like vines—familiar, subtle, tightening slowly. Deferred decisions sat in the corner of his mind like unopened bills, stacked and ignored. He told himself it wasn't the right time. He told himself he'd get around to it. He told himself he was fine.

That's the thing. Statistics provide a variety of numbers, and we are not sure which one is correct, but the average adult tells many lies each day. Most are to themselves.

He was no exception.

He found himself exhausted—not just physically, but soul-tired. Every decision came with emotional weight. Every pursuit of "more" gave him less and less in return. It was the law of diminishing returns, and he was living it. The next purchase, the next affirmation, the next distraction ... none of it delivered what it promised. He finally had to ask: What is the cost of staying on this path? And what might the benefit be if I let go?

That was the moment of awakening.

It didn't happen all at once. But he started small—telling the truth to himself. He acknowledged the lies, the attachments, the avoidance. And then he did something radical in a world that celebrates hustle and comparison: He reset.

He began to see that contentment wasn't passivity—it was power. It took tempered resilience to stay grounded when everything around him demanded performance. It took courage to say no to one thing in order to say yes to something better.

The healing came gradually, like the turning of a dial. He practiced gratitude. He aligned his choices with his values. He recalibrated daily. And in that rhythm, he found something surprising: peace.

Not the loud, fireworks kind of peace. But the deep, durable peace that says you already have enough. You already are enough.

He cut the cord, and discovered a life he hadn't known was waiting.

Don't you want to be like him? Don't you want his story to be your story?

Reflection & Questions: Cutting the Cord and Reclaiming Contentment

We often don't realize how tightly we're holding on—until the weight starts pulling us under. Deferred decisions, distorted truths, emotional attachments, and false promises of "more" can quietly wear down our peace and joy.

Ask yourself the following questions to pause, reflect, recenter.

- What emotional attachments or old habits might be quietly draining your contentment? Are you holding onto something you once needed but no longer serves your soul?
- Where are you telling yourself small lies to avoid change or discomfort? What truth might set you free if you had the courage to face it?

- Consider your personal "cost-benefit" landscape. Is the time, energy, or emotional toll worth the return you're getting?
- What decisions have you been deferring? Could one small act of clarity or closure bring peace today?
- Where might you need a reset? A course correction? A cut cord? Contentment often begins with subtraction.
- How can you build tempered resilience—grit that's guided by grace? Instead of running harder, what would it look like to rest deeper?
- Can you name one area in life where you are choosing truth, clarity, and simplicity over noise, avoidance, or comparison? Celebrate that. That's contentment in motion.

Contentment is a Daily Choice

The more we choose these practices, the more we become the kind of people who live contented lives—not because everything is perfect, but because we've trained our hearts to see what matters.

So start small.

Start today.

Start again tomorrow.

You don't have to change everything overnight. You just have to begin.

Here's something different we can call it: course correction.

Course Correction: Returning to Contentment

In aviation or navigation, a course correction is a simple but crucial adjustment—realigning a journey that has drifted slightly off course. It doesn't require shame or panic, only the awareness that even a few degrees off, left unattended, can lead to an unintended destination.

You don't have to be far off track to need a course correction. A pilot just a few degrees off from the intended flight path can end up hundreds of miles from the destination. But a small adjustment—early, intentional—can make all the difference.

The same is true in the journey toward contentment.

We often don't recognize how we've drifted until we feel anxious, jealous, unsatisfied, overwhelmed. Sometimes it's because we've been scrolling too much. Or we've been measuring our lives by someone else's timeline. Or we've believed the lie that doing more or having more or becoming more will finally make us feel enough.

Course correction isn't about guilt. It's about grace. It's noticing the drift and deciding to respond—not with panic, but with peace and humility. It's saying, "I may have wandered, but I can come back."

What does a course correction look like in everyday life?

- Turning off the noise and sitting quietly with God, even if it's just five minutes.
- Putting down the phone when you start comparing your life to someone else's highlight reel.
- Letting go of a good opportunity that isn't good for your soul.
- Saying no so you can rest.
- Saying yes to something that brings life, even if it's small and simple.

Course correction is a spiritual practice. It's repentance in the most hopeful sense—returning, reorienting, realigning with the truth of who God is and who you are. It's admitting that discontentment has pulled you off track, but contentment is still within reach. It's the intentional act of recognizing when your current path is leading you away from your values, purpose, or peace—and choosing to realign your direction.

What if today is a course correction? Not a grand overhaul, not a dramatic transformation. Just a small, quiet decision to realign with the path of peace, gratitude, and presence.

It requires humility to admit you're off track, clarity to know what matters most, and courage to return.

Many people drift from contentment not because of one big decision but through small compromises, busyness, resentment, comparison, or misplaced priorities. A life once grounded in grace becomes restless. A soul that once delighted in simple gifts now longs for what it doesn't have. But the invitation of contentment is always open—it's not too late to come back.

Scriptures That Reflect Course Correction:

- *"Trust in the LORD with all your heart and lean not on your own understanding; in all your ways submit to him, and he will make your paths straight."* (Proverbs 3:5–6)

  Trust leads to redirection.

- *"Whether you turn to the right or to the left, your ears will hear a voice behind you, saying, 'This is the way; walk in it.'"* (Isaiah 30:21)

  God gently nudges us back to the path.

- *"Your word is a lamp for my feet, a light on my path."* (Psalm 119:105)

  God's Word reveals where course corrections are needed.

- *"If one of you should wander from the truth and someone should bring that person back...."* (James 5:19–20)

  Course correction can be personal or communal.

- *"When he came to his senses...."* (Luke 15:17–20)

  The prodigal son realized his emptiness, returned, and found welcome, not punishment.

Course Correction Isn't a Failure—It's a Gift.

Each time we notice we're drifting, we're offered a moment of clarity and grace. That awareness is evidence that God is still speaking, still guiding, still offering contentment. And it's never too late to return.

A Contentment Course Correction

Sometimes living a life of contentment isn't about staying perfectly on course—it's about making small, humble adjustments along the way.

Here are a few course corrections we can practice:

- We recalibrate when we've drifted from gratitude. Gratitude anchors us. When we lose it, even slightly, a recalibration helps us notice what we already have.
- We pivot when chasing "more" isn't working. Ambition can become addiction. Contentment often calls for a pivot away from endless striving and back toward simple joy.
- We reset when anxiety has built up too much. Anxiety clouds our view. A healthy reset—rest, prayer, perspective—clears the way for peace to return.
- We realign with God's promises when comparison creeps in. Comparison distracts us from God's unique work in our lives. Realigning with His truth restores contentment.

Contentment isn't perfection. It's a life of continual course corrections—always moving closer to the heart of God.

INTERLUDE: THE JOURNEY AHEAD

> *"I decided to write a book on contentment, not because I have contentment figured out and consider myself the most contented person in the world. Rather, I began to study and ultimately to write about contentment because I am often discontented."*
>
> **—William B. Barcley**[26]

Contentment is not the end of the road.

It is the road.

And you are still walking.

Up to this point, we've paused. We've looked inward. We've wrestled with disappointments, limits, comparisons, and unfulfilled dreams. We've explored gratitude and generosity, stillness and surrender. And we've discovered—sometimes slowly, sometimes in surprising clarity—that contentment isn't a moment we arrive at. It's a way of moving through life.

But now we ask: What's next?

Because even when we learn to be content with what we have, we still have jobs to do. We still belong in families, serve in communities,

26 William B. Barcley, *The Secret of Contentment* (Phillipsburg, NJ: P&R Publishing, 2010), 9.

dream about the future, and try to discern what to do with the years we've been given. Contentment doesn't stop us from growing—it frees us to grow from the right posture.

This is the journey ahead.

To carry contentment into our relationships—not demanding from others what they cannot give, but offering love from a full place.

To bring contentment into our sense of calling—not chasing applause, but serving with quiet purpose.

To hold contentment in our dreams—not giving up, but trusting that God writes better stories than we do.

We don't leave contentment behind. We take it with us. We take it into each conversation, each decision, each ordinary day. We learn that contentment isn't complacency or settling.

It's strength. It's clarity. It's trust.

So, take a deep breath.

What if the life you're meant to live flows from a contented heart?

Let's keep walking—into relationships, into purpose, into tomorrow—holding this quiet truth: You don't have to strive for what you already carry.

Contentment is your companion for the journey ahead.

Moving Toward Peaceful Joy in a Hi-Tech, Overwhelmed World

In a culture of short attention spans and endless notifications, contentment feels counterintuitive. Here are steps to reclaim it:

1. **Silence the Noise:** Turn off your devices. Take five minutes daily to sit in silence, letting your soul catch its breath.
2. **Practice Gratitude:** Start or end each day with three things you're thankful for. Gratitude rewires the brain for joy.

3. **Slow Down:** Say no to unnecessary commitments. Walk slower, eat slower, think slower. Contentment thrives in unhurried moments.
4. **Simplify:** Declutter your home, schedule, and heart. Let go of what doesn't matter to focus on what does.
5. **Seek Real Connection:** Share a meal without screens. Listen deeply. Contentment grows in relationships, not followers.
6. **Rediscover Sabbath:** Set aside one day to rest, worship, and trust God's provision. Sabbath recalibrates our hearts for contentment.

Practical Ways to Live with More Contentment

1. **Practice Gratitude Daily.** Make a habit of listing things you are thankful for each day, whether in a journal or prayer. Gratitude shifts focus from what's lacking to what's abundant.
2. **Limit Comparisons.** Avoid comparing your life to others' lives, especially on social media. Instead, focus on your own journey and progress.
3. **Simplify Your Life.** Declutter your home, schedule, and commitments. Simplicity helps you appreciate what you already have and reduces stress.
4. **Focus on the Eternal.** Reflect on spiritual truths that remind you of God's provision and sovereignty. Trust that He knows and provides what you truly need (Matthew 6:31–33).
5. **Live Within Your Means.** Avoid debt and practice financial stewardship. Learn to distinguish between needs and wants to cultivate satisfaction with what you have.
6. **Serve Others.** Helping others shifts your focus from your own challenges to the joy of making a difference. Acts of kindness foster gratitude and humility.
7. **Develop Contentment as a Discipline.** Contentment doesn't happen automatically. Make an intentional effort to

accept your circumstances and trust God's plan in every season.

8. **Spend Time in Prayer and Reflection.** Regular prayer and meditation on God's Word can bring peace and contentment. Scriptures like Philippians 4:11–13 or Psalm 23:1 remind us of God's sufficiency.
9. **Focus on Relationships Over Possessions.** Invest in meaningful connections with family, friends, and your community rather than material goods or achievements.
10. **Celebrate Small Wins.** Take time to acknowledge and enjoy small victories or blessings in your day-to-day life.
11. **Practice Mindfulness.** Stay present and savor the moment instead of worrying about the past or future. Mindfulness helps you appreciate life as it is right now.
12. **Replace Complaints with Praise.** Each time you're tempted to complain, pause and find something to praise instead. This rewires your mindset toward positivity.
13. **Learn the Value of Contentment Through Trials.** Difficult circumstances can teach us to depend on God and grow in trust. Reflect on how past struggles led to unexpected blessings.
14. **Limit Exposure to Consumerism.** Reduce time spent watching ads or browsing online stores that create unnecessary desires. Instead, focus on activities that nurture your soul.
15. **Rest in God's Provision.** Memorize and meditate on promises such as Hebrews 13:5: "Never will I leave you; never will I forsake you." Trust that God provides exactly what you need in His timing.

By implementing these practices, you can nurture a heart of contentment and experience greater peace and joy in your daily life.

Daily Neuroplasticity for Contentment

1. **Gratitude Journaling:** Begin and end each day with three things you're thankful for—training your brain to focus on abundance rather than lack.
2. **Intentional Pauses:** Throughout the day, take 60 seconds to breathe deeply, pray, or recite a calming Scripture.
3. **Reframing Thoughts:** When hindrances arise, pause and name them. Replace them with truths—"I am enough in Christ" or "God's grace is sufficient for this moment."
4. **Joyful Movement:** Walk outside, stretch, or dance. Movement shifts our focus from stress to joy, rewiring our emotional state.
5. **Connection:** Speak words of encouragement to someone and let their gratitude feed your soul. Contentment is contagious.

Each day has its challenges, its distractions, and its hindrances. But each day also offers a gift: the opportunity to choose contentment. Through small practices, rewired thoughts, and Spirit-led rhythms, contentment becomes less of a fleeting feeling and more of a way of life.

SECTION FOUR
A LIFE OF LASTING CONTENTMENT

20 CONTENTMENT IN RELATIONSHIPS

"When Jesus said the last shall be first, and the least shall be great, and the slave the greatest of all, he wasn't giving orders. He was simply describing the truth about God's kind of community and how different it looks from the way things generally work in our world." **—John Ortberg**[27]

We tend to underestimate how much our discontent is shaped by our relationships. The people closest to us influence how we think, feel, and respond—sometimes more than we realize.

But the influence runs both ways. The condition of our heart also shapes the condition of our relationships. When contentment grows deep within, it changes how we love, how we speak, and how we respond even in seasons when others cannot—or will not—reciprocate.

Our discontent can just as easily shape our relationships, for better or worse. The attitudes we bring into our connections with others often determines whether those bonds grow stronger or strain when under pressure.

Discontentment hides in comparison, in unmet expectations, in frustration when people don't meet our needs or fulfill our hopes. It creeps in when someone else's success makes us question our worth. It grows

27 John Ortberg, *The Life You've Always Wanted: Spiritual Disciplines for Ordinary People* (Grand Rapids, MI: Zondervan, 2015), 120.

when their silence feels like rejection, when their blessing feels like our lack.

But contentment invites us to see people differently.

It helps us lay down the pressure to fix, to compete, to prove. It creates space for us to enjoy people rather than measure ourselves against them. Instead of chasing affirmation or carrying bitterness, we learn to choose presence. We learn to love from a place of fullness, not need.

I used to think peace in relationships came from everything being smooth. No conflict. No tension. Everyone doing what I needed them to do. But that's not contentment. That's fantasy.

Real contentment shows up in the mess and the misunderstanding. It whispers peace in a conversation that stings. It helps you forgive when the apology never comes. It steadies you when the people you lead don't seem to notice how hard you're trying.

I've had to learn this slowly. Through disappointment. Through grief. Through seasons when I wanted to walk away from the people that God called me to love.

Contentment kept me there. Not stuck, but steady.

And I'm still learning.

There's freedom in choosing to show up as you are, even when others don't understand. There's strength in blessing someone else without needing to be praised in return. There's deep joy in listening without interrupting, in laughing without competition, in giving without strings attached.

When we stop striving for perfect relationships, we can begin living with peaceful ones.

There's no need to pretend. No need to constantly adjust our behavior to win approval. We can let people be who they are and trust God to be who He says He is.

Sometimes that means staying when we want to leave. Sometimes it means letting go when we want to control. Sometimes it means speaking grace instead of defending ourselves. Sometimes it means saying nothing and simply being present.

This is how contentment lives in our relationships: Through presence, humility, gratitude, and grace. Through choosing to believe we are enough—even when others make us feel like we're not. Through remembering we are loved—even when others forget to say it.

What if that's the starting point for peace? Not changing others, but choosing contentment in how we show up to love them.

Let's be honest: We can't fix all the relational tension in our lives. But we can live with less striving. We can love with less fear. We can rest in the truth that our value doesn't come from how others see us—but from how God sees us.

Let contentment guide your relationships. Let it silence comparison. Let it interrupt resentment. Let it soften your heart and your words.

Because contentment isn't just something we find in solitude—it's something we offer in community.

We tend to underestimate how much our discontent is shaped by our relationships. But living with contentment deep within can create a calmness so steady that what others do—or not do—cannot rob us of it. Amid scars, across the lips, among the wounds, love stays. Like winds and storms blowing all around, contentment in relationships brings love like the calmness in the eye of a hurricane.

Choosing Love Again and Again

The calendar moves faster than we expect. One day blends into the next until suddenly we find ourselves at the edge of a new beginning. A marriage counting anniversaries. A friendship deepening. A decision to stay when walking away would be easier.

Love is beautiful. But real love—the kind that builds a life, the kind that sees and stays—is more than a ceremony or a feeling.

Contentment doesn't mean settling for a fairytale. It means finding deep joy in the sacred ordinary. In the private choices. In the consistent prayers. In the vows that are lived out while needing sleep and finishing the laundry and facing disagreements and paying bills with little money available and voicing words of peace during dinner after a hectic day.

True contentment in relationships is this: being proud not of the highlight reel, but of the hearts being built quietly along the way.

It's about the faith lived in the ordinary.

It's about prayers whispered in parking lots, and grace offered when tempers flare.

It's about laughter that keeps a home alive, and tears that remind us we're not alone in the ache.

And it's about praying—often. Together. Alone. When it makes sense. When it doesn't. Letting prayer become the rhythm of a shared life, not just a rescue call in emergencies.

Worship when it's easy. Worship more when it's not.

Serve not because you have to, but because you've discovered the joy in giving.

Let Jesus be more than a name spoken during a ceremony. Let Him be the center—not just of your delightful days, but your everyday.

Let His love be your foundation. Let His grace shape your words, your patience, your forgiveness.

Invite mentors to speak truth. Receive their coaching, their caring. Invite friends into your messes and your miracles. And become safe places for others, too.

And never let go of childlike faith. Keep it near, right beside you. Let it decorate your home with hope.

Most of all, remember what love really is:

Love is patient—when the lines are long, when healing takes time, when silence needs space.

Love is kind—not just in public smiles but in private conversations, in daily choosing gentleness over irritation.

Love celebrates the other's wins. It listens. It learns. It lets go of scorecards.

Love is not easily angered. It doesn't store bitterness in the attic of memory.

Love protects with time and loyalty. Love rebuilds trust. Love speaks hope with trembling voices.

And love keeps going—on ordinary Wednesdays and during sleepless nights. On days when the dream feels far away. On days when the joy finally feels real.

This love doesn't fade.

It grows deeper with every sacred moment, every kind nod, every genuine yes. Every hard decision to forgive. Every act of choosing to stay.

This is covenant. This is contentment in relationship.

And this—this kind of love—is a testimony. Not just to the world around you. But to your own hearts. A testimony that what you've been searching for may already be yours.

Living without Contentment

Living without contentment can have significant consequences across many aspects of health, including psychological, mental, physical, relational, and spiritual well-being. The following are possible consequences for Physical Heath and Relational Well-Being

Physical Health

The absence of contentment can lead to various physical health issues. Chronic loneliness, for example, has been found to increase the risk of cardiovascular diseases, high blood pressure, and obesity. It can also elevate cortisol levels leading to anxiety, depression, digestive problems, heart disease, sleep disturbances, and weight gain.

Relational Well-Being

Discontentment can strain personal relationships, leading to social isolation and a lack of meaningful connections. This isolation can create a self-reinforcing cycle, where loneliness begets further social withdrawal, exacerbating feelings of discontent.

Why So Many Live without Contentment

- People often set their hopes on temporary goals and possessions that were never meant to satisfy eternal needs.
- Comparison—especially through social media—leads to a constant feeling of being behind or not measuring up.
- Many chase outward success while neglecting inward health, purpose, and relationships.
- Unrealistic cultural expectations and pressure to perform leave both men and women weary and empty.
- When we tie our worth to career achievement, beauty, status, or busyness, contentment slips away unnoticed.
- Suppressed emotions, especially in men, and unrealistic standards, especially for women, contribute to dissatisfaction.
- Many carry unresolved trauma or unmet emotional needs that fuel a deep sense of restlessness.
- Young people feel trapped by fear—of rejection, of not being enough, of the unknowns about their future.
- Older adults often face loneliness, fading identity, physical limitations, and fear about finances or death.

- Even those who appear successful battle a quiet craving for more—more approval, more recognition, more control.
- We often fail to see purpose in the present—missing the sacred in ordinary moments like folding laundry or caring for others.
- There's a deep spiritual hunger behind the dissatisfaction—a longing for belonging, purpose, healing, and peace that only God can provide.
- Until we see life from His perspective, contentment will remain elusive—no matter our age, stage, or status.

21 CONTENTMENT AND CALLING

"The things we do, do something to us; they get into the core of our being and shape our loves and longings." **—John Mark Comer**[28]

When our sense of *calling*—our God-given purpose, direction, and contribution to the world; our sacred assignment; our unique role in God's story—becomes cluttered with too many options, too many comparisons, or too many expectations, our thoughts start to spiral. We overthink every decision, dissect every result, replay every conversation, and rehearse every possible outcome. The mind runs not toward clarity, but into anxious loops—repeating worries that spiral into more worry and distraction. We become trapped in negative thought patterns, haunted by past regrets or gripped by future anxieties. We don't feel called anymore. We feel cornered.

But contentment invites us to take another way.

It reminds us that calling isn't about pressure; it's about presence. Not a constant climb, but a faithful step. Not a performance, but a practice of showing up with gratitude and grace.

That's where grounding practices come in—spiritual disciplines that calm the chaos and help us reconnect to what matters most. In moments when our calling feels foggy, metacognition—thinking about

28 John Mark Comer, *Practicing the Way: Be with Jesus, Become Like Him, Do as He Did* (Colorado Springs, CO: Waterbrook, 2019), 98.

our thinking—can help. Anticipatory metacognition practice helps us identify potential pitfalls before they become problems. Our selective attention becomes key: where we focus, we'll follow.

Neuroscience is the way to go here—not as a rival to faith but as a companion. Our brains offer the ability to change. Neuroplasticity[29] allows us to rewire our thoughts and behaviors, putting us in partnership with the Spirit to cultivate peace. We can move toward mental satisfaction, but not mediocrity. We can live with satisfaction, but not complacency.

Focus on the positive changes you wish to implement. Practice daily gratitude. Build competence by celebrating what you can do rather than what you haven't done yet.

Contentment in calling means this: We trust God enough to stay the course, even if the crowd isn't cheering and the path is quiet. It means we let go of the need for "abundance of possessions" or applause (see Luke 12:15) and instead seek the abundance of obedience.

Because when we live that way, calling becomes less about where we're going and more about how we're getting there and Who is guiding each step.

Living Fully in the Life You've Been Given

What if contentment is not the enemy of calling, but the soil it grows in?

We often confuse ambition with purpose. We think fulfilling our calling means constantly climbing, constantly expanding, constantly proving we're doing something significant. But the truth is, your calling doesn't need noise to be real. It needs faithfulness. It needs roots.

You don't have to chase a platform to have a purpose. You don't need an audience to live a meaningful life. You don't need to be recognized to be obedient.

Contentment helps you stay where your feet are—so your soul can catch up to your schedule. It gives you permission to be present in the small things, knowing they often become the sacred things.

29 *The American Heritage Dictionary of the English Language*, 5th edition, defines neuroplasticity as the ability of the brain to change in structure or function in response to experience.

The lie says, "If you settle here, you'll miss out." The truth says, "If you always chase there, you'll miss what God is doing here."

Let that sink in.

Calling isn't always about going. It's often about staying—staying faithful, staying humble, staying aware of God's presence in your present circumstances, staying near the small, staying with the unknown. It's not a formula or a finish line; it's a journey of trust.

How do we practice contentment in our calling?

1. **Redefine Success.** Success isn't always more. Sometimes it's deeper.

   Are you loving well? Serving faithfully? Remaining honest? Then you are succeeding—whether or not it goes viral or gets applause.

2. **Embrace Limits.** Limits are not failures; they are invitations. Boundaries, capacity, even "no" can become sacred ground when we view them through the lens of contentment. God can do more through a surrendered limit than an overextended life.

3. **Celebrate the Ordinary.** Answer the email with kindness. Write the message no one sees. Pray for the person who may never know you prayed. That's where calling lives—in the quiet, ordinary, everyday moments of obedience.

4. **Stay Curious, Not Competitive.** Someone else's success doesn't cancel your calling. Let their growth inspire you instead of intimidating you. Ask, "What is God teaching me here?" not, "Why am I behind them?"

5. **Let Joy Lead You.** Joy is a compass for calling. It shows up when you're aligned. When you're writing, speaking, leading, building, healing, helping, serving—whatever it is you were made to do—and it resonates deep in your chest, follow that joy. Joy doesn't mean it's easy. But it often means it's right.

6. **Stay with God, Not Just the Goal.** If your dreams take you further from God, they are not dreams worth chasing. Let His presence define your purpose. He is not impressed by your résumé. He is moved by your dependence.

A few lines to carry with you:

- Your calling is not a race. It's a rhythm.
- The place you are may not be the place you dreamed of—but it might be the place you're needed.
- Contentment is not resignation; it is rootedness.
- Don't confuse visibility with value. God sees the quiet work.
- You are not behind. You are becoming.

We often want a map, but God gives us manna. Daily strength. Daily grace. Just enough light for the next step.

So take that step. Be faithful with today. Plant yourself where you are. Speak with love. Listen with intention. Build slowly. Trust deeply. Rest freely.

Your calling isn't somewhere far away.

It's right here, waiting to be lived with joy, with trust, and with contentment.

Living in Contentment: A Week's Journey

Sunday:

The rush to worship can steal the rest of worship. We wake early, dress in our best (or these days, however we want), and run toward the sacred—but sometimes forget the sacred is already here. Contentment finds us when we let Sunday slow us down, not speed us up. Today, remember that Sabbath is not a list to complete but a love to receive. Rewire your brain by practicing stillness—sit longer in the sermon of silence and hear the whisper of God.

Monday:

The grind begins again. Mondays bring expectations, plans, and the pressure to perform. The hindrance is this lie: "Do more, and you'll be enough." Instead, rewire your thinking by starting with gratitude. Write down three things that went well yesterday, then look for three new blessings today. Contentment on Mondays grows when we trust God for the week ahead, one task at a time.

Tuesday:

The weight of what's unfinished sets in. Tuesday's hindrance is impatience, the voice that says, "You should be further along by now." Choose instead to pause and refocus—step away from the noise and breathe. Use neuroplasticity by speaking truths to yourself: Progress is happening, even when I can't see it. Contentment thrives when we trade frustration for faithfulness.

Wednesday:

Midweek exhaustion hits and the temptation to compare arises—your success versus someone else's shine. The hindrance is comparison, which kills joy and blinds us to what God is doing here and now. To rewire your brain, spend time noticing beauty. Look outside, walk barefoot, or thank God for the intricate details of His creation. Contentment on Wednesdays grows in the art of noticing.

Thursday:

Thursdays often feel monotonous, a repeat of tasks and routines. The hindrance is boredom, the false belief that life must be extraordinary to be meaningful. Rewire your brain by finding joy in small victories—celebrate what you finished no matter how small, and thank God for sustaining grace. Contentment learns to sing in the ordinary, not just the extraordinary.

Friday:

The week's end nears, but unresolved conflicts or unmet goals linger. Friday's hindrance is regret—the voice that whispers, "You could've done better." Counter it by practicing forgiveness, starting with yourself. Rewire your mind by journaling what you've learned this week and thanking God for His mercies. Contentment grows when we release the past and look forward with hope.

Saturday:

The day of rest often turns into the day of rush—errands, plans, and the busyness of "free time." The hindrance is distraction, pulling us in every direction except peace. Rewire your brain by intentionally practicing presence—put down your phone, listen deeply to loved ones, and savor the moment. Contentment blossoms when we live fully in today.

Helpful Quotations on Contentment

The following authors have thought deeply about contentment, and this is what they have to say:

> *"Contentment is the direct fruit of having no higher ambition than to belong to the Lord, at His disposal."* **—Megan Hill**[30]

> *"Christian contentment is that sweet, inward, quiet, gracious frame of spirit, which freely submits to and delights in God's wise and fatherly disposal in every condition."* **—Jeremiah Burroughs**[31]

> *"Contentment is learned as Christ's power enables us to rejoice in him above all earthly treasures."* **—Andrew M. Davis**[32]

---

30 Megan Hill, *Contentment: Seeing God's Goodness* (Phillipsburg, NJ: P&R Publishing, 2018), 45.

31 Jeremiah Burroughs, *Contentment, Prosperity, and God's Glory* (Grand Rapids, MI: Reformation Heritage Books, 2013).

32 Andrew W. Davis, *The Power of Christian Contentment: Finding Deeper, Richer, Christ-Centered Joy* (Grand Rapids, MI: Baker Books, 2019), 106.

"True contentment is found not in having everything we want but in trusting that God is everything we need." **—Jennie Pollock**[33]

"Contentment is the inward, gracious, quiet spirit that joyfully rests in God's providence." **—Erik Raymond**[34]

"Contentment is the art of accepting and embracing the life God has given us, finding peace in His provision."

—Anne Woodcock[35]

"Contentment comes when we can honestly say with the psalmist, "The Lord is my shepherd; I shall not want." **—Eugene Peterson**[36]

"If we are to learn contentment, we have to be able to spot discontentment. If we are grumbling, bitter, or worrying, then we can be sure we are discontent." **—Erik Raymond**[37]

"The shortness of life allows us to see that most things in this life are trivial and only a few things really matter." **—Allen Hunt and Matthew Kelly**[38]

"Remember always that this loving God suffered for us and suffers with us still. It is safe to trust Him in the storm, to have contentment in His will, and to wait for understanding until later."

—Richard A. Swenson[39]

---

33 Jennie Pollock, *If Only: Finding Joyful Contentment in the Face of Lack and Longing* (Epsom, Surrey, England: The Good Book Company, 2020),74.

34 Erik Raymond, *Chasing Contentment: Trusting God in a Discontented Age* (Wheaton, IL: Crossway, 2017), 23.

35 Anne Woodcock, *Contentment: Healing the Hunger of Our Hearts* (Epsom, Surrey, England: The Good Book Company, 2008).

36 Eugene H. Peterson, *Leap Over the Wall: Earthy Spirituality for Everyday Christians* (San Francisco, CA: HarperSanFrancisco, 1997), 96.

37 Raymond, *Chasing Contentment*, 128.

38 Allen Hunt and Matthew Kelly, *The Fourth Quarter of Your Life: Embracing What Matters Most* (Cedaredge, CO: Wellspring, 2022), 7.

39 Richard A. Swenson, *Contentment: The Secret to a Lasting Calm* (Colorado Springs, CO: NavPress, 2013), 188.

> *"Letting go of control is about holding on to a rough vision of your life, but keeping yourself open to all the detours, to the intuitive nudges."* —**Jamie Varon**[40]

These quotes offer diverse perspectives on contentment, emphasizing trust in divine providence, the cultivation of inner peace, and the recognition of life's inherent gifts.

Insights About Contentment

John Mark Comer contributes the following insights about contentment:

- "Contentment is living in such a way that your unfulfilled desires no longer curb your happiness."
- "The solution to an overbusy life is not more time. It's to slow down and simplify our lives around what really matters."
- "Too much time spent in the past leads to depression; too much time spent in the future leads to anxiety. Live in the moment."
- "Hurry and love are oil and water; they simply do not mix."
- "An easy life isn't an option; an easy yoke is."[41]

These insights from Comer encourage embracing the present, simplifying life to focus on what truly matters, and understanding that true contentment comes from aligning one's desires and pace of life with deeper values and relationships.

40 Jamie Varon, *Radically Content: Being Satisfied in an Endlessly Dissatisfied World* (Beverly, MA: Quarto Publishing Group, 2022), 165.
41 John Mark Comer, *The Ruthless Elimination of Hurry: How to Stay Emotionally Healthy and Spiritually Alive in the Chaos of the Modern World* (Colorado Springs, CO: Waterbrook, 2019), 216, 62, 33, 23, 88.

22 CONTENTMENT OF THE FUTURE

"[Contentment] frees you to work hard and trust God with the results, knowing that God is sovereign over all hidden factors."
—David Kaywood[42]

I don't often write or teach about the Book of Revelation. But as we near the end—of this book and, more importantly, as we continue learning contentment as a way of life—this feels like the right place to pause and listen.

Let's call this moment what it is: "A Conversation with John: A Reflection on Revelation 21:1–6."

I closed my eyes and imagined sitting across from the old apostle. His face weathered, yet generous. His eyes sharp, yet kind. He had seen things most of us never will—and lived long enough to carry the weight of both suffering and hope.

"John," I said, "you saw a new heaven and a new earth. You saw the end of all things, and the beginning of everything we were made for. What would you say to us now?"

He didn't hesitate.

42 David Kaywood, *A Call to Contentment: Pursuing Godly Satisfaction in a Restless World* (Fearn, Scotland: Christian Focus Publications Ltd., 2024), 109.

"Live with hope," he said. "The world you see now—the pain, the brokenness, the losses—they are not the end. I saw the One on the throne, and He said, 'I am making everything new.' Everything. New. That includes you."

I nodded slowly, but the pain of my questions lingered. "But how do we keep going when the waiting feels long? When life doesn't make sense, when contentment feels out of reach?"

John looked at me with the quiet assurance of someone who had suffered deeply and loved faithfully.

"Remember who holds the story," he said. "I was exiled when I saw the vision. Isolated. Forgotten. But God wasn't silent. He pulled back the curtain so I could see what was still true. That He was with His people. That He still is with His people. That one day there will be no more death, no more tears, no more mourning. And that day is coming."

He paused, then said, "You don't need to escape the present to find peace. You just need to anchor yourself in the future that's already promised. The God who will dwell with you then is already dwelling with you now. The future isn't far off—it's pulling you forward."

I sat in silence, letting his words settle.

And then he added softly, "Be content not because life is easy, but because the ending is sure. Your story isn't over, and your joy isn't finished."

Stillness in the Promise

Contentment isn't found in having everything now. It's found in trusting the One who holds everything—past, present, and future. When we set our eyes on the new heaven and new earth, we stop measuring our lives by what we lack and start living in the light of what we've been promised. The ache doesn't disappear, but the non-stop-every-thought fear does. Because we know the end of the story, and it's beautiful.

It's beautiful because of *Who* writes it.

- The Author and Finisher of our faith (Hebrews 12:2).
- Our Shepherd who restores our soul (Psalm 23:1–3).
- Our Father who gives good gifts (Matthew 7:11).
- Our Refuge and Strength (Psalm 46:1).
- The One who began a good work in us and will be faithful to complete it (Philippians 1:6).
- The One who promised, "I will never leave you or forsake you" (Hebrews 13:5).
- The God who wipes every tear from our eyes (Revelation 21:4).

When we remember *Who* He is, we rest in *what* He has promised. Our contentment is no longer fragile, depending on the day's headlines or the outcome of our plans. It's anchored in His unchanging character. And that anchor holds, even in the fiercest storm.

Hopeful Hearts in an Uncertain Tomorrow

The future is one of the greatest enemies of contentment—not because the future is bad, but because we try to live in it before it arrives.

We obsess over what's next.

We stress over what might happen.

We predict, plan, prepare, and worry.

We live five years ahead in our minds while today slips silently through our hands.

We take that book of Revelation and we turn it into something we can clearly explain and define—in our attempts at controlling words that were never intended to be seen the way we look at them.

But contentment is not control. Contentment is not fully understanding everything. Contentment calls us back. It calls us to now. To this breath. This meal. This conversation. This decision. This glance. This tempo. This song. This story. This ordinary miracle of a moment.

Contentment doesn't ignore the future—it simply puts it in its place.

The future matters. But it isn't here yet. And when it arrives, it will do so as the present—not a problem to fix, not a storm to fear.

Contentment doesn't deny reality. It chooses trust instead of fear. It chooses stillness instead of scrambling. Jesus said,

> *"Do not worry about tomorrow, for tomorrow will worry about itself. Each day has enough trouble of its own."* (Matthew 6:34)

He wasn't telling us to ignore our responsibilities. He was freeing us from our obsession with control.

We often think control will bring us peace. But it's actually the illusion of control that causes the most anxiety. When we finally admit we're not in charge—and we don't have to be—we breathe deeper.

Contentment shifts our posture toward the future in three ways:

1. **It slows us down.** We stop rushing through life like it's a race to win. We start receiving life as a gift to be unwrapped slowly, gratefully, faithfully.

2. **It strengthens our trust.** We remember Who holds tomorrow. We rest in the God who has never once abandoned His people—even when their tomorrows looked dark.

   Revisit biblical stories of Joseph, Ruth, Daniel, Mary, and Paul. They all stepped into uncertain futures with a certain God.

3. **It shapes our hope.** Hope isn't pretending everything will be easy. Hope is knowing God is already in the future, preparing a way, providing strength, working good—even through what we don't yet understand.

Some practical ways to live content in the face of the unknown:

- Pray your fears instead of rehearsing them.
- Talk to God about your what-ifs. Let His peace meet you where your fear lives.
- Keep a journal of provision.
- Write down how God showed up in past seasons. Let your history with Him shape your confidence for the future.
- Anchor yourself in today's faithfulness.
- Focus on what you can do today: love, serve, rest, create, connect. Be fully here before trying to figure out what's next.
- Memorize promises, not predictions.
- We don't know how everything will unfold, but we know the One who goes before us. "I will never leave you or forsake you" (Hebrews 13:5). That's a promise you can carry anywhere.
- Let go of the timeline.
- God is never late. He's never in a rush. And He's not bound by your calendar. Contentment lets you live free from artificial pressure.

A few lines to hold onto:

- The future is in God's hands. You don't need to carry it all.
- Waiting is not wasted time when you wait with faith.
- Hope grows when you trust more than you plan.
- You can be content and still be curious about what's next.
- Contentment isn't settling—it's standing strong in what you know is true even when you don't know what comes next.

You're not called to live obsessed with the future. You're called to live with faith now. And if you live with trust today, you'll meet tomorrow with peace—not panic.

Let contentment meet you here, so hope can greet you there.

The future will come. But for now, stay. Stay present. Stay grounded. Stay content.

Wonder in the Waiting

My wife, Debbie, and I planned a vacation—just the two of us, a few restful days in North Carolina during the summer. But plans changed. Debbie's mom was placed in the hospital so we had to cancel.

We waited. And later, when the time was right, we decided to make a smaller trip happen—a few October days in Dillard, Georgia.

We left on a Thursday morning, grateful for the opportunity and determined to make this one work.

Our first stop was Clayton. We strolled the sidewalks of the small town, talked with people, looked around, and shopped a little. Then we drove to one of my favorite places—Tallulah Gorge. I walked the steps down and back up again. All 1,099 of them. I stopped at the bridge to stare at the water, to listen, to breathe. Waterfalls invite me to pause; I accepted the invitation.

Then Debbie and I walked together across the top of the gorge, loving the view from above.

We drove on to Dillard, ate dinner, and rested for the night. The next morning greeted us with crisp mountain air in the 40s, the kind that refreshes your lungs and slows your pace.

At breakfast we listened to a man nearby telling his life story—loudly, passionately, unfiltered. We smiled, listened, reading each other's minds, and simply enjoyed being there.

Later, we drove through the mountains toward Highlands, North Carolina. The trees showed off their October colors. We walked. We talked. We ate lunch outside in the cool breeze, coats zipped. We wandered through shops too expensive to buy from, but valuable for the views, the laughter, and the moments shared.

We stopped at Dry Falls and walked to the base, then under the falls. The sound of the rushing water filled the air. I stood there like a child again, feeling the mist and the wonder.

The drive back was slower—I unintentionally took the long way. But the long way might not always be the wrong way. We saw more color, more light, more evidence of beauty still happening. That night we found a small Mexican restaurant, heard fireworks from a nearby football game, read, walked, prayed, and felt grateful.

The next morning we had breakfast at the Dillard House. It was under construction as new owners were bringing changes. But the food? Still delicious. The view? Still breathtaking.

That contrast stayed with me: the gorgeous mountain views beside the broken buildings and construction equipment. The stars and planets above. The leaves changing. The clouds drifting by. Beauty and brokenness side by side.

It reminded me of life.

The Dillard House is still, as I write this, under construction. And the Dillard House still offers a fascinating view of mountains.

Changes in life aren't always either/or. Sometimes they're both/and.

Beauty, awe, and wonder can still exist amid change. When old things are torn down, new things are built. When roads are messy and blocked, transformation is happening underneath.

Change brings limited roads and firm fences. It brings waiting and frustration, confusion and anticipation. But even there—wonder is on the way. And during the waiting, beauty is still here.

That's the future of contentment: learning to live in the middle of what God is still making. Trusting that what's unfinished is not unworthy.

It's best to welcome both—the present and the future. The here and now, and the soon to come.

If nothing changes, then nothing changes. But during the change, there's still wonder in the waiting.

Notice it. Welcome it. The view is still an invitation to remember there's good all around us.

The work isn't finished—but the wonder's already here.

A Modern Call for Contentment

Jonathan Haidt, author of The Anxious Generation, again offers insight. Haidt and many other voices show that our modern struggle with contentment isn't inevitable. By stepping away from the cultural forces that fuel dissatisfaction and leaning into practices that promote rest, connection, and gratitude, people can find a way forward. These works remind us that true contentment is countercultural—and that's precisely why it's so valuable.

Sadness and grief are undeniable parts of life. Disappointments, losses, and unfulfilled dreams weigh heavily on our hearts, leaving us questioning how we can choose contentment amid such struggles. Yet, contentment doesn't mean denying pain; it means finding peace and trust in the presence of God, even in sorrow. Here are ways to integrate grief and sorrow into a life of contentment:

1. Acknowledge the Pain.

Contentment doesn't ignore suffering—it embraces honesty about how hard life can be. The Psalms are full of raw emotion, like Psalm 42:3 where the writer laments, "My tears have been my food day and night." These words show us that it's okay to weep, to feel the weight of life's struggles.

Practical Step: Give yourself permission to grieve. Talk to God about your pain, journaling prayers of lament and asking Him to meet you in your sorrow.

2. Seek God's Presence in the Storm.

In the midst of life's greatest trials, contentment can grow when we focus on God's presence. Psalm 34:18 reminds us, "The Lord is close to the brokenhearted and saves those who are crushed in spirit." Even when circumstances feel unbearable, God is near.

Practical Step: Spend time in quiet prayer or worship, inviting God to be with you. Sometimes His peace comes not through answers but through the comfort of His presence.

3. Let Grief Deepen Your Perspective.

Pain often changes the way we see life. It reminds us of what truly matters and teaches us to find joy in the small, everyday blessings. Jesus Himself wept over loss (John 11:35) but also pointed to a hope beyond this world.

Practical Step: Each day look for one thing to be thankful for, even if it's small—a kind word, a warm drink, or a moment of rest. Gratitude doesn't erase grief but can coexist with it.

4. Cling to Hope amid Loss.

When dreams die or loss seems insurmountable, contentment comes from anchoring ourselves in the eternal hope God promises. Revelation 21:4 speaks of a future where "there will be no more death or mourning or crying or pain." This promise doesn't invalidate our present pain but assures us that it's not the final word.

Practical Step: Meditate on passages that remind you of God's eternal promises. Let them lift your perspective above temporary circumstances.

4. Share the Burden.

Sadness can isolate, but contentment grows when we let others walk with us in our grief. Galatians 6:2 encourages us to "carry each other's burdens." Community provides strength and reminds us that we're not alone.

Practical Step: Reach out to trusted friends, a pastor, or a counselor to share your struggles. Sometimes, contentment comes through the love and support of others.

5. Embrace Sorrow as a Teacher.

Ecclesiastes 3:4 reminds us that there's "a time to weep and a time to laugh." Both seasons are part of a full life. Contentment isn't about avoiding sadness but allowing it to shape us with wisdom and compassion.

Practical Step: Reflect on how your pain has deepened your understanding of life or helped you empathize with others. Consider how God might use it for growth.

6. Rest in God's Sovereignty.

Contentment comes when we release control and trust that God is still working, even when life feels shattered. Romans 8:28 assures us, "In all things God works for the good of those who love him."

Practical Step: When facing loss, pray for the strength to surrender your plans to God. Ask Him to help you trust His greater purpose, even if it's not yet clear.

7. Find Peace in the Present Moment.

When overwhelmed by sadness or fear of the future, grounding ourselves in the present can nurture contentment. Jesus said, "Do not worry about tomorrow" (Matthew 6:34), reminding us that today has enough for us to handle.

Practical Step: Practice mindfulness by focusing on one moment at a time. Notice your breath, the sounds around you, or the beauty of nature. Let these moments remind you of God's care.

A Hopeful Conclusion

Contentment doesn't erase grief, but it transforms it. It allows us to hold sorrow in one hand and trust in the other. As Psalm 30:5 declares, "Weeping may stay for the night, but rejoicing comes in the morning."

Grief shapes us and sadness seasons us, but neither has the final word. By leaning into God's presence, trusting His promises, and finding gratitude in the midst of pain, we can discover a contentment that anchors us even in the hardest seasons.

23 THE PRACTICE OF CONTENTMENT

"We can be asking for good things with good motivations, but if we've reached the point where the desire for them is making us discontent, we need to make a choice." **—Jennie Pollock**[43]

Contentment is more than a mood.

It's more than a moment of peace during a perfect sunset. It's a practice, a lifestyle.

We practice contentment when we choose joy in the middle of waiting. We practice contentment when we celebrate the success of others instead of comparing ourselves. We practice contentment when we show up for ordinary days with extraordinary gratitude.

It's not a switch you flip. It's a path you walk.

Sometimes with confidence. Sometimes with a limp.

But still, you walk.

43 Jennie Pollock, *If Only: Finding Joyful Contentment in the Face of Lack and Longing* (Epsom, Surrey, England: The Good Book Company, 2020), 94.

You keep practicing contentment ...

- When prayers go unanswered.
- When no one notices your efforts.
- When life feels unfair.
- When tomorrow looks uncertain.
- When your strength feels small.

That's when it matters most.

Some practices are easy to identify: prayer, gratitude, generosity, simplicity. But there's another practice—one that's not usually listed in spiritual disciplines. It's the practice of staying open when life doesn't move smoothly.

It's the practice of contentment in awkward transitions.

Awkward Transitions

I should have a smooth segue from the previous sentence to this line. But if I did, it wouldn't fit the point.

So, welcome to the floundering.

We—or at least I—tend to view awkward transitions as negative experiences. Interruptions. Unplanned, unprepared, and unexpected encounters that don't fit my preferred script. I like knowing in advance. I prefer preparing well. I like estimated times with smooth openings, closings, and steady progress.

Like a song with fitting verses, chorus, and bridge. Like a sermon with a clear introduction, solid points, key takeaway lines, fitting illustrations, and an inviting conclusion. Like a dinner with dessert after the meal. Like a ball game with innings or quarters appropriately in order.

But life isn't like that. And contentment can come amid life's strange rhythms.

What should we do?

Welcome the awkward transitions of life. Find contentment in the uneven surfaces, in the uncomfortable stuttering, in the moments that last too long or end too soon, in the sounds that are too loud or too soft.

Call it life. And find contentment there—amid the chaos, among the interruptions, around the awkward transitions.

What's next might not notify us in advance. It might not grab the mic on cue. It might just arrive, stand before us, and invite us into an unexpected endeavor.

Welcome the we-did-not-expect-this. It might be the very *this* we need the most.

A Vision of Enthusiastic Contentment

Imagine waking up, not with dread, but with anticipation, not because every circumstance is perfect but because your soul is at rest in God. Imagine working hard, not for applause, but for the joy of serving the Kingdom. Imagine finding moments of delight in the ordinary—a child's laughter, a bird's song, a quiet evening at home choosing to go nowhere else.

Contentment isn't passive; it's active trust. It's choosing to anchor your heart in the unchanging love of the Father, the saving grace of the Son, and the sustaining power of the Spirit. It's a daily surrender of striving for success and instead seeking the Kingdom. It's the peace that passes understanding, guarding your heart and mind in Christ Jesus (Philippians 4:7).

In this world of striving, let us be people of stillness. In this culture of dissatisfaction, let us be people of gratitude. And in this life of brokenness, let us be people of hope. For in contentment, we find the abundant life God has always wanted for us.

Contentment is rooted in deeper soil than circumstances. It grows best in hearts that are anchored—anchored in God's love, not culture's noise. Anchored in grace, not performance. Anchored in truth, not trends.

Now What?

I've heard all the definitions and explanations. I've read the information and illustrations. I've gathered data, studied the material, written and rewritten the convictions I hope to share. But here's the harder question—what will I do myself?

Will I live with deep inner contentment when thoughts and emotions push back? Will I rest in true contentment when nothing seems to go how I hoped, how I prayed, how I thought it needed to go?

The many months of studying and writing this book have been my way of learning what contentment really is—and what it isn't. The work has helped me design a biblical strategy to welcome it, and to hold myself accountable to apply it.

It hasn't been overwhelming or condemning. It hasn't been burdensome or legalistic. It's been inviting. Freeing. Welcoming. Transforming.

This process has given—and still gives—me a better view of life. It's an invitation to pause, not overreact. It's a case for an abundant life seen from a wider window than self-centeredness allows. It's faith that sees beyond the visible, hears beyond the audible. It's a walk toward potential, while cherishing each step of the journey. It's a practice of refusing to be controlled by circumstances while also refusing to control those circumstances.

It's waking up thankful. Living the day grateful. Ending the night with deep breaths, thankful thoughts, and a soul at rest.

Isn't that better? Isn't that the route worth taking? Stepping forward with a grin, a nod, a wink, a gaze ahead. Not controlled by scars, damage, mistakes, or fears. Aware of them, but facing them appropriately. Choosing contentment as a way of life—not just hearing, studying, writing, or researching about it, but receiving it from its Creator.

Let's do that. As we turn the pages of this book and as we walk the stages of this life, let's do that. Let's receive contentment from its Creator.

You don't have to be more to be enough.

You are not missing out on your life. You are not behind. You are not unseen. You are not forgotten.

If you've learned anything through these chapters, let it be this: Contentment isn't something you stumble into. It's something you choose.

Every single day.

You don't have to feel it first. You don't need all the answers. You just need to take a step. To breathe. To whisper a prayer. To slow down. To thank God. To sing along with a song. Then play it again and sing along again. To pay full attention in a conversation. To stare at that tree, that river, that cloud, that rainbow, that friend. To taste and digest the food slowly. To serve someone. To rest well.

You don't have to earn contentment. You get to receive it.

Because God already offers it.

Integrating into a Life Strategy

We can turn these steps into part of a personal strategy by:

1. **Setting Intentions:** Regularly review these practices and align them with His values and faith.
2. **Reflecting Often:** Using journaling or conversation with trusted friends to evaluate how we're practicing contentment.
3. **Celebrating Wins:** Marking milestones of growth in contentment, whether in small moments of gratitude or big shifts in mindset.

Read and Study These Scripture Passages About Contentment

1. *"I am not saying this because I am in need, for I have learned to be content whatever the circumstances. I know what it is to be in need, and I know what it is to have plenty. I have learned the secret of being content in any and every situation, whether well fed or hungry, whether living in plenty or in want. I can do all this through him who gives me strength."* (Philippians 4:11–13)

2. *"But godliness with contentment is great gain. For we brought nothing into the world, and we can take nothing out of it. But if*

we have food and clothing, we will be content with that." (1 Timothy 6:6–8)

3. *"Keep your lives free from the love of money and be content with what you have, because God has said, 'Never will I leave you; never will I forsake you.'"* (Hebrews 13:5)

4. *"The LORD is my shepherd; I lack nothing."* (Psalm 23:1)

5. *"So do not worry, saying, 'What shall we eat?' or 'What shall we drink?' or 'What shall we wear?' For the pagans run after all these things, and your heavenly Father knows that you need them. But seek first his kingdom and his righteousness, and all these things will be given to you as well."* (Matthew 6:31–33)

Goals and Scripture

1. **Pursue Big Dreams and Believe in the Big:**
   - *"Now to him who is able to do immeasurably more than all we ask or imagine, according to his power that is at work within us."* (Ephesians 3:20)
   - *"Delight yourself in the Lord, and he will give you the desires of your heart."* (Psalm 37:4)
2. **Have Huge Faith:**
   - *"If you can believe, all things are possible to him who believes."* (Mark 9:23, NKJV)
   - *"For we live by faith, not by sight."* (2 Corinthians 5:7)
3. **Work Hard and Commit to Hard Work:**
   - *"Whatever you do, work at it with all your heart, as working for the Lord, not for human masters."* (Colossians 3:23)
   - *"Lazy hands make for poverty, but diligent hands bring wealth."* (Proverbs 10:4)

4. **Take Risks and Endure:**

    - *"Be strong and courageous. Do not be afraid; do not be discouraged, for the Lord your God will be with you wherever you go."* (Joshua 1:9)
    - *"Let us not grow weary in doing good, for at the proper time we will reap a harvest if we do not give up."* (Galatians 6:9)

5. **Find Internal Peace:**

    - *"Peace I leave with you; my peace I give you. I do not give to you as the world gives. Do not let your hearts be troubled and do not be afraid."* (John 14:27)
    - *"The Lord gives strength to his people; the Lord blesses his people with peace."* (Psalm 29:11)

Practical Principles

1. **Pursue Big Dreams:**
    - Write your vision down and pray over it (Habakkuk 2:2).
    - Take intentional, small steps toward big goals without letting fear of failure paralyze you.
    - Surround yourself with people who encourage and challenge your vision.
2. **Have Huge Faith:**
    - Feed your faith with Scripture and testimonies of God's greatness.
    - Speak your faith aloud, affirming God's promises daily.
    - Look for God in the small victories as He leads you toward the big ones.
3. **Work Hard and Commit to Hard Work:**
    - Set realistic goals and manage your time wisely.
    - Use your talents and strengths fully, remembering you're a steward of God's gifts.
    - Rest intentionally, understanding that rest fuels better work.
4. **Take Risks:**
    - Remember that faith often requires stepping into the unknown, trusting God's leading.
    - Evaluate risks prayerfully and seek wise counsel before acting.
    - Celebrate courage, even if the outcome isn't what you expected.

5. **Endure:**
    - Stay grounded in God's promises during seasons of waiting or trial.
    - Find joy in the journey, not just the destination.
    - Reflect on past seasons where God's faithfulness brought you through.
6. **Find Internal Peace Amid the Effort:**
    - Start and end each day with quiet moments of prayer or reflection.
    - Practice gratitude as a way to counter stress and negativity.
    - Use Scriptures such as Philippians 4:6–7 to release anxiety to God.
7. **Laugh and Celebrate the Journey:**
    - Keep a sense of humor even in challenging times as a way to stay lighthearted.
    - Celebrate small victories as steps toward bigger dreams.
    - Share joy with others, building a community of hope and positivity.

CONCLUSION: YOU ALREADY HAVE WHAT YOU'RE LOOKING FOR

> *"He seemed like a symbol of a time and a place gone by. A simple guy who appeared content with where he was in life. Something those of us who are so driven often struggle with."*—**Chris Myers**[44]

During a recent appointment with my counselor, I felt like I had come full circle. We reflected on our meeting six months before when he quietly handed me one word to carry into the year: contentment.

Since then, I read. I researched. I journaled. I prayed. I started writing this book. But more than that, I tried to live it.

He listened as I talked about my various jobs, responsibilities, relationships, and daily realities. He heard me mention stress, confess concerns, and acknowledge uncertainties. But then he smiled. "I can see it," he said. "You're not pretending. You're living with more peace. You're learning the life of contentment."

The moment lingered in silence that felt settled. The same mountains stood outside the window—familiar now, less watchful, almost at peace.

44 Chris Myers, *That Deserves a Wow: Untold Stories of Legends and Champions, Their Wins and Heartbreaks* (New York: William Morrow and Company, 2024)

That moment felt like another unexpected dessert—not earned or even anticipated, just offered. Quiet. Sweet. Enough.

Not because I'd mastered the subject—but because I had let the truth sneak in. I didn't have to manufacture it. Peace didn't wait for everything to be perfect. It simply showed up.

He noticed. I noticed.

And I want that for you. I want you to notice.

I want you to know what it's like when joy sneaks out of your words. When peace shows up uninvited but welcomed. When contentment no longer feels like a concept but becomes a quiet companion.

If you made it this far, something inside you longs for what contentment offers.

Maybe you're tired of the race. Tired of the pressure. Tired of being told you're not enough.

And maybe—finally—you're ready to believe a better story: You were never meant to find your worth in performance, productivity, popularity, or possessions. You were made for more. More presence. More peace. More joy. More Jesus.

Contentment doesn't mean you stop growing.

It means you stop striving for an identity you already have.

You stop running toward a peace that's already been given.

This is your invitation: Let go of the lie that you must be more to matter. Step off the treadmill of not-enough. Slow down. Breathe deeply. Remember who you are and whose you are.

Jesus said, "I have come that they may have life, and have it to the full" (John 10:10).

That's what contentment is—a full life, not a full calendar. A full heart, not a full schedule. A soul at peace, even when the world is chaotic.

Let your story become one of quiet strength. Of deep joy. Of steady presence. Of sacred ordinary.

Let your story become one of lasting contentment.

Because we don't need to feel like we're falling behind. We can be exactly where we need to be. And we already have what we're looking for.

Now, let's go live like it.

Holy Spirit-Inspired Solutions

The Holy Spirit offers guidance, comfort, and wisdom to shift our hearts from striving to resting in God:

1. **Shift from Striving to Surrender.**
    - **Solution:** Acknowledge that we are not in control and that true contentment comes from God.
    - **Scripture:** *"Come to me, all you who are weary and burdened, and I will give you rest."* (Matthew 11:28)

      "Be still, and know that I am God." (Psalm 46:10)
    - **Application:** Spend daily time in prayer, asking the Holy Spirit to reveal areas of misplaced striving. Surrender those areas to God.
2. **Seek God's Perspective on Success.**
    - **Solution:** Redefine success as faithfulness rather than achievement.
    - **Scripture:** *"Seek first his kingdom and his righteousness, and all these things will be given to you as well."* (Matthew 6:33)

      "The Lord will accomplish what concerns me." (Psalm 138:8, NASB 1995)
    - **Application:** Regularly ask, "Am I being faithful to God's call in this season or am I chasing my own agenda?"
3. **Embrace Rhythms of Rest and Work.**
    - **Solution:** Live in step with the Holy Spirit's rhythms, which include both diligent work and restorative rest.

- **Scripture:** "Six days you shall labor and do all your work, but the seventh day is a sabbath to the Lord your God" (Exodus 20:9–10).

  "In repentance and rest is your salvation, in quietness and trust is your strength." (Isaiah 30:15)
- **Application:** Set aside a weekly Sabbath and daily moments for stillness and reflection. Ask the Holy Spirit to help you honor these times.

4. **Prioritize Relationships Over Results.**
   - **Solution:** Remember that people and relationships reflect God's priorities more than tasks or goals.
   - **Scripture:** *"Do nothing out of selfish ambition or vain conceit. Rather, in humility value others above yourselves."* (Philippians 2:3)
   - **Application:** Create intentional space in your schedule to connect with loved ones and serve others without rushing.
5. **Practice Gratitude in the Present.**
   - **Solution:** Focus on what God is doing right now instead of constantly striving for the future.
   - **Scripture:** *"Give thanks in all circumstances; for this is God's will for you in Christ Jesus."* (1 Thessalonians 5:18)
   - **Application:** Keep a gratitude journal. Start and end each day thanking God for specific blessings.
6. **Walk by Faith, Not Comparison.**
   - **Solution:** Celebrate others' success without letting it diminish your own journey.
   - **Scripture:** *"Each one should test their own actions. Then they can take pride in themselves alone, without comparing themselves to someone else."* (Galatians 6:4)
   - **Application:** Focus on obedience to God's unique calling for your life, trusting that His path for you is enough.

7. **Rest in God's Peace.**
   - **Solution:** Let the Holy Spirit guard your heart and mind, silencing anxiety and striving.
   - **Scripture:** *"You will keep in perfect peace those whose minds are steadfast, because they trust in you."* (Isaiah 26:3)

     "The fruit of the Spirit is love, joy, peace...." (Galatians 5:22)
   - **Application:** Meditate on God's Word, praying for the Holy Spirit to fill you with His peace daily.

The Invitation

The Holy Spirit calls us not to abandon hard work, big dreams, or bold faith, but to do these things in partnership with Him. This means:

- Trusting God with the results.
- Finding joy in the process, not just the outcomes.
- Balancing effort with surrender.

True contentment is found not in what we achieve but in who we become as we walk with Christ, empowered by the Holy Spirit.

Contentment for Today's World

Throughout the Book of Acts, Paul's epistles, and David's Psalms, we learn that contentment isn't circumstantial; it's spiritual. It's about trusting God, resting in His presence, and rejoicing in His goodness.

In our hi-tech, distracted, and dissatisfied culture, let's pause to listen to these ancient voices. Let's learn to wait like the apostles, trust like Paul, and pray like David. For in their stories, we find a roadmap to the peace, joy, and contentment our restless hearts long for.

The Acts of Contentment

The Book of Acts is more than a history lesson. It's an invitation to live a life shaped by the Spirit, where contentment isn't tied to outcomes but to obedience. Each chapter offers a glimpse of what contentment looked like for the early church—living faithfully, trusting God, and rejoicing in His presence amid the uncertainties of their journey.

- **Acts 1:** Contentment in waiting. The disciples stayed together, praying, trusting Jesus' promise of the Holy Spirit. They waited—not idly but expectantly. Can we learn to find peace in God's timing, trusting that His plans will unfold as they should?
- **Acts 2:** Contentment in community. They broke bread, prayed, and shared their possessions. Contentment was not in hoarding but in giving, not in independence but in interdependence. What could our lives look like if we found contentment in sharing, not striving?
- **Acts 3:** Contentment in the name of Jesus. Peter and John didn't have silver or gold, but they had something greater: the power of Jesus' name. Contentment isn't found in what we have, but in who we know.

- **Acts 4:** Contentment in boldness. Threatened by authorities, the early believers prayed for courage, not escape. Contentment isn't avoiding trouble; it's trusting God in the midst of it.
- **Acts 5:** Contentment in integrity. Ananias and Sapphira remind us of the dangers of discontentment—the temptation to present a false version of ourselves. True contentment is found in living honestly before God and others.
- **Acts 6:** Contentment in serving. The apostles delegated responsibilities, content to focus on prayer and teaching. The early church thrived because they understood contentment comes from fulfilling our unique calling, not doing it all.
- **Acts 7:** Contentment in faithfulness. Stephen's story shows us that even in suffering, contentment is possible when we fix our eyes on Jesus.
- **Acts 8:** Contentment in the unexpected. Philip found himself in the wilderness, but there he met the Ethiopian eunuch. Contentment trusts that God is at work, even in the detours.
- **Acts 9–28:** Over and over we see contentment in action—Paul preaching in prisons, believers rejoicing in persecution, and the church growing despite opposition. Contentment wasn't about their circumstances but about their confidence in God.

Paul's Letters: A Roadmap to Contentment

Paul wrote his letters to guide, correct, and encourage. But woven through each epistle is an invitation to live in contentment, not as passive resignation but as active trust in God.

- **Romans:** Contentment in God's sovereignty. Paul reminds us that God is working all things for good (Romans 8:28). Contentment grows when we trust that His plans are higher than ours.
- **1 & 2 Corinthians:** Contentment in weakness. Paul boasts in his weaknesses, knowing that God's power is made perfect there (2 Corinthians 12:9). Can we find joy in our limitations, trusting God's strength?
- **Galatians:** Contentment in freedom. True contentment isn't in legalism, but in the freedom of Christ (Galatians 5:1).
- **Ephesians:** Contentment in unity. Paul emphasizes the beauty of the church united in Christ. Contentment thrives in community, not comparison.
- **Philippians:** The manifesto of contentment. As I've written, Paul writes, "I have learned the secret of being content" (Philippians 4:11). It's not about what we have but about who strengthens us.
- **Colossians:** Contentment in Christ's sufficiency. In Him we are complete (Colossians 2:10, NKJV). Contentment begins when we stop striving to fill ourselves with what only He can provide.
- **Thessalonians, Timothy, Titus, and Philemon:** In each letter, Paul encourages believers to trust God, work hard, and live holy lives. Contentment is a byproduct of faithfulness.

David's Psalms: The Songs of Contentment

David, the shepherd-king, wrote songs that reflect the ups and downs of life. Through his Psalms, we find prayers of contentment—anchoring us in God's presence, promises, and faithfulness.

- **Psalm 23:** Contentment as the Lord's sheep. David declares, "The Lord is my shepherd; I lack nothing" (v. 1). Contentment is trusting the Shepherd's care.
- **Psalm 27:** Contentment in seeking God. "One thing I ask of the Lord ... that I may dwell in the house of the Lord all the days of my life" (v. 4) Contentment comes from prioritizing His presence.
- **Psalm 46:** Contentment in chaos. David writes, "Be still, and know that I am God" (v. 10). Even when the world crumbles, contentment is found in stillness before Him.
- **Psalm 51:** Contentment in confession. David's repentance shows us that contentment isn't perfection; it's living humbly before God.
- **Psalm 63:** Contentment in the wilderness. David's soul thirsted for God more than water in the desert. Contentment grows when God becomes our greatest need.

DISCOVER MORE CONTENTMENT

This book includes access to additional resources including video teaching, audio, workshops, and community!

Just click on the Access Code below to discover how the book in your hands can become a portal to a new discovery experience!

ABOUT CHRIS MAXWELL

Chris Maxwell is a husband, father, and grandfather. He is a writer, pastor, poet, spiritual life director, international speaker, and a man who loves people. Chris hopes to be a voice of encouragement through words spoken, words written, and a life lived.

Website/Blog: chrismaxwell.me

Twitter: @CMaxMan

Instagram: cmaxman

Facebook: Facebook.com/PausewithChrisMaxwell

Email: CMaxMan11@gmail.com

Books by Chris Maxwell

Beggars Can Be Chosen: An Inspirational Journey Through the Invitations of Jesus

Changing My Mind: A Journey of Disability and Joy

Unwrapping His Presence: What We Really Need for Christmas

Pause: The Secret to a Better Life, One Word at a Time

Pause for Moms: Finding Rest in a Too Busy World

Pause for Pastors: Finding Still Waters in the Storm of Ministry

Pause with Jesus: Encountering His Story in Everyday Life

Underwater: When Encephalitis, Brain Injury, and Epilepsy Change Everything

a slow and sudden God: 40 years of wonder

embracing now: pain, joy, healing, living

Equilibrium: 31 Ways to Stay Balanced on Life's Uneven Surfaces

Things We've Handed Down: Twelve Letters I Leave for You

Contentment: What You're Searching for Is Already Yours

www.ingramcontent.com/pod-product-compliance
Lightning Source LLC
LaVergne TN
LVHW010651110826
845149LV00014B/3028

9781971560021